"The authors lead us to a clear yet overlooked truth: nurses have been the leaders in healthcare innovation long before doctorpreneurs and engineers laid claim to that right. Creating 'work-arounds' and on-the-fly solutions in a system that constantly presents barriers to delivering care for their patients, nurses are natural innovators. This book will help them gain their rightful seat at the entrepreneurs' table."
Sanaz Cordes, MD, serial entrepreneur and CEO of DotCom Therapy.

"The Nurse's Guide to Innovation *is a seminal comprehensive must-read and essential guide for nurses at any career level interested in catalyzing their entrepreneurial innovative spirit. This book provides a thoughtful and engaging roadmap to the challenging landscape of healthcare innovation. Readers will find these insights invaluable as they prepare to make their own contribution to transforming healthcare through innovation."*
Michael Petersen, MD, Health Innovation Lead, Accenture

"The most prolific entrepreneurs carefully choose which problems to solve, and that requires a deep understanding of those problems. Nurses have always been closest to understanding health and illness through the lens of the whole person: mind, body, and spirit. Now is the time to use that deep personal experiential knowledge of human needs and unsolved problems and apply the emerging exponential technologies to address those needs in meaningful ways. This book is a treasure trove of both 'How to Get Started' and 'How to Succeed.' Even the most experienced entrepreneurs will find new insights in this compendium of practical 'how to' information sourced from the masters themselves."
John Mattison, MD, Assistant Medical Director, CMIO, emeritus

The Nurse's Guide to Innovation

By Bonnie Clipper
Mike Wang
Paul Coyne
Vince Baiera
Rebecca Love
Dawn Nix
Wayne Nix
Brian Weirich

Foreword by Shawna Butler, RN, MBA

SUPER STAR press

E-mail: info@superstarpress.com
20660 Stevens Creek Blvd., Suite 210
Cupertino, CA 95014

Published by Super Star Press™, a THiNKaha® imprint
20660 Stevens Creek Blvd., Suite 210, Cupertino, CA 95014
http://superstarpress.com/

First Printing: August 2019
Paperback ISBN: 1-60773-124-X   978-1-60773-124-5
eBook ISBN: 1-60773-123-1   978-1-60773-123-8
Place of Publication: Silicon Valley, California, USA
Paperback Library of Congress Number: 2019907650

Trademarks

Warning and Disclaimer

Dedication

This book is dedicated to all those who are trying to change the world, in the hope that they may positively experience their own innovation journey.

Contents

"The difficulty lies not so much in developing new ideas as in escaping from old ones."

—John Maynard Keynes

This is an exciting era to be a nurse! The convergence of fast-moving mobile technologies, big data, and open platforms has enabled a permission-free environment for nurses to unleash their natural instincts to problem solve, experiment, invent, rapidly iterate, and innovate. We are truly in a technology renaissance, and nurses (20 million across the globe) are jumping in to shape new roles, new patient experiences, redesigned workflows, care models, devices, policies, protocols, and digital solutions and establish themselves as essential partners in the transformation and democratization of access to health, care, and treatment.

Innovation is at the core of the nursing profession. It's part of our DNA, genetically linked to Florence Nightingale, the English social reformer, statistician, and founder of modern nursing. Her contributions, boldness, and brilliance cannot be overstated. Every hospital and healing environment today is a reflection of her "radical" nursing innovations. She set the stage for nurse-led innovation, inspired generations of nurse innovators, and provided several case studies on being an influencer and gamechanger.

Nurses have a lot of ideas about improving health experiences and outcomes because they see and understand the unmet needs and are constantly fixing the gaps in care. Nurses go to the dark, difficult, dangerous places to care for the hard-to-reach and hardly reached. Their close observation of people in their living environments, lifestyle routines, and interaction with care systems and processes helps nurses zoom into the root problem and come up with clever and novel solutions. While nurses have a huge pool of insights and are perfectly situated to shape and accelerate innovation, it's hard and overwhelming to know where to begin.

To convert their clinical and practical insights into value-creating innovations, nurses need encouragement, resources, specific how-tos, and a tribe of supporters willing to share what they've learned and mistakes they've made so more and better solutions succeed and improve people's lives. This timely, optimistic, and detailed guide offers just that.

The Nurse's Guide to Innovation is the playbook and toolkit for health and care innovation. It is written for the front-line wave makers, the system change agents, those who quietly and loudly question the status quo, and the relentless problem solvers, rebels, activists, path breakers, troublemakers, and bold innovators. It's also for the innovation cheerleaders, fans, opponents, and champions. Innovation is a team sport. Take your position and get started.

Do not wait for permission.

Do not wait for an invitation.

Proceed until apprehended.

Shawna Butler, RN, MBA

Faculty, Medicine & Neuroscience, Singularity University, Exponential Medicine, USA
EntrepreNURSE-in-Residence, REshape Center for Health(care) Innovation, Radboud University Medical Center, Netherlands

1 Introduction

By Dawn Nix & Wayne Nix

Objectives:

By the end of this chapter, the reader will be able to:

- Explain the differences between innovation and invention.
- Evaluate the value of an idea.
- Describe how motivation can help with advancing ideas.

"Dream big. Start small. But most of all, start."
— *Simon Sinek (Sinek, 2015)*

I have an idea, now what?

Congratulations. In exploring this book, you've taken the first step toward innovation. Now, what's the next step? How many more steps are there? In exploring this book, you've taken the first step towards innovation. What is innovation versus just "being innovative"? We have all asked ourselves questions such as these at one time or another. We crafted this book with a simple goal in mind: to help nurses, just like us, get off to the best start possible advancing their ideas and maybe even generating revenue, aka making money. This is a road map to help increase your odds for success along the innovation journey, a guide we ourselves wish we had.

Please note, we realize that this is only a guide—it is our opinion and is based on lessons we have learned, successes and failures we have experienced, and evidence we have gathered. We do not claim this to be a "step by step," "a, b, c," or "1, 2, 3" type of guide.

Being on the innovation journey is similar to providing patient care or practicing nursing. Not everything is black and white, workflows are often non-linear, and there are many shades of gray. However, our team of authors contains nurse innovators and entrepreneurs, and you will have a better grasp of the possibilities of innovation, as well as a basic understanding of how to effectively navigate your innovation journey. Be forewarned: it will not be easy. However, it will likely be life changing and fun.

"What you seek is seeking you."

— Rumi, thirteenth-century philosopher (Rumi, n.d.)

What is an idea?

What are ideas? How valuable are they? Where do they come from? Why are some more creative than others? Many questions remain, and here is our attempt to answer a few of them. To start with, an idea "is a formulated thought or opinion" (Merriam Webster, n.d.) and results from our intrinsic traits of creativity. As humans, we often envision new and better ways of doing things, and at one time or another, we try to "connect the dots." This is especially true as nurses; we almost can't help ourselves from doing the "dot connecting." We can all think of times where we tried to think through something and ended up considering whether it could be better in the future.

Chances are, we can all quickly name a number of things that can be improved even in our own lives. What makes certain individuals better at "connecting dots" and being innovative is closely related to their ability to be creative. Johansson (2006) suggests that one can maximize their creative potential once they "strike a balance between depth" and "breadth of knowledge" (p.5). Research suggests that three components are required for creativity, including an overlapping of expertise, creative thinking skills, and motivation (Kumar, 2012). The combination of these factors will effectively provide the "right" environment for creativity to occur.

Identifying a "valuable" idea

Consider what an idea is worth. Usually it's worth zilch, nada, a big goose egg, because ideas by themselves hold little value. Ideas may demonstrate that an individual is clever, although the ideas themselves rarely hold much intrinsic value. In fact, many ideas are actually bad ones. Have you ever done something you regret? Sure, we all have. Good ideas become valuable once they are implemented or actually "brought to life." However, this is only if they prove viable or can transcend from the imagination state. Determining an idea's "value" will help in the decision of whether to move forward and consider advancing the idea into a business plan or even implementing it.

What criteria determine a good idea, and how will one know where to focus the effort to generate such an idea? There are a few simple questions to help determine the value and opportunity that may exist within an idea, with a goal of balancing a clever idea with an actionable one. Pursuing innovation for the sake of innovation is pointless and wasteful, and a goal of healthcare overall is to decrease waste. Answering these questions early will provide guidance as to whether the idea is worth pursuing.

The next step is to determine how the idea might be accomplished. To gain support, the idea must be feasible and, dare we say, profitable. Idea "value" often has a financial connotation and relates to whether it will generate revenue, or "make money." The earlier that value can be determined, the better this will gain momentum to continue the forward progress. Evaluating an idea generally includes careful consideration of the following:

- Does it solve a problem, meet a need, or fill a gap? If the answer is NO, stop here.
- Is it novel?
- Is there competition? Who? Is it a crowded market?
- Is there clinical prudence (existing evidence, efficacy, safety, likelihood to produce improved outcomes, etc.)?
- Does it demonstrate the ability to reduce costs or generate revenue through sales?
- Does it suggest the likelihood of securing funding?
- Does this demonstrate the outlook to secure reimbursement and identify a successful pricing strategy?
- Does it have an optimistic marketing potential (branding, communication, public relations, etc.)?
- Is manufacturing/production feasible (prototyping, engineering, etc.)?
- Are logistics and distribution feasible?

After mulling over these questions, it is up to you to determine if the idea has "value" or is worth your time and effort to continue with it. Moving ideas along the phases of a business plan brings inherent risk of failure. If you believe that going ahead with this idea is worth the risk of failure, realize that failure of innovation or of an idea is not failure of self. If you decide that this idea is ready to be turned into reality, the next step is to move it along the continuum to make it real. This process will be described as you read through this book, as it involves thinking like an innovator and entrepreneur, writing a business plan, protecting your ideas or intellectual property (IP), and learning how to secure funding, how to brand and market, and how to engage on the innovation journey.

Skill-building exercise

Evaluate an idea that you have been thinking about. Write it down, and identify answers to the questions above. See how well your idea fares as it makes it through this filtering process.

What is invention?

People invent products every day. An invention is "something invented, such as a device, contrivance, or process originated after study and experiment" (Merriam-Webster, n.d.). Workarounds are often invented as a means to fill in a gap or simplify a complex process. Workarounds are also referred to as positive deviances. A positive deviance "is an intentional act of breaking the rules for a greater good" (Gary, 2012, p.2). Nurses often need to develop workarounds in order to provide safe, timely, and quality patient care.

An example of how hospitals and other organizations are encouraging invention among employees is through "makerspaces," or innovation labs, in order to help clinical staff build or prototype solutions that may fill system/process gaps. This is a great solution for many who desire to roll up their sleeves to develop or prototype their idea/invention—and it's fun! Those wishing to invent more purposefully typically follow a more structured pathway/process to create their product or service. Generally, this process advances by identifying solutions and working through the solutions until the best, most feasible solution emerges. Remember that just because you have created something in your basement, that doesn't mean it brings value to others.

Here are further questions to determine whether an idea is worth moving through the invention pathway:

- Would anyone else benefit from your invention?

- Can you protect your invention?

- Do you expect to be compensated?

- Does the product/process need an internal board review or FDA clearance?

- How will you get your brilliant idea to market (aka practice acceptance and/or commercialization)?

Why pursue innovation?

Why do we work toward innovation? Generally, it's to make our lives and our work better/easier, to improve the care we provide, and to make the world a better place. In case you haven't noticed, our world would benefit from some improvement, even transformation—especially in how we handle overall health, wellness, and the delivery of care.

Whether you are just entering the nursing profession or are a seasoned veteran nurse, we should "do" more than just ponder. As nurses, we are trained to be inquisitive, ask questions, and challenge what we see. It's part of our skill set, part of our "critical thinking mindset." What's missing is the next step of "critical rethinking" and then "implementation." To "do" anything requires a "why." Often, the "why," or the "true" reason that innovation is sought and fought for, is to satisfy our humanistic "want." Even those claiming to innovate for altruistic reasons are doing so to satisfy an individual, instinctual emotional desire of "want."

> *"Do or do not, there is no try."*
>
> — Yoda (Kurtz, 1980)

The importance of motivation

Yoda's quote is related to commitment toward a result. What Yoda did not say was that to "do" anything, it must first be important or "matter." Understanding your own motivation, your own passion, and your own "wants" is a key factor for all those who work toward the complex and ever-shifting landscape of innovation. Many educational theorists believe motivation to be the most important virtue to an individual's success: "Even more than particular cognitive abilities, a set of motivation attributes, childlike curiosity, intrinsic interest, perseverance bordering on obsession, seem to set individuals who change the culture apart from the rest of humankind" (Nakamura & Csikzentmihaly, 2015, p.196).

As nurses, we learned about Maslow's Hierarchy of Needs, which suggests that after basic physiological needs are met, other things are also desired as "wants" (Burton, 2017). You may "want" love and esteem, or you may "want" to perform the best you can in your career. When you "want" to make a difference in others' lives, it may be to satisfy and make a difference in your own life. Why not "want"? Don't we *all* deserve better? But we cannot "want" things into existence. We have to *do*. This requires motivation, and understanding your motivation and goals will help you stay resilient to the many challenges that lie ahead as an innovator. In order to move ahead, it is important to understand what innovation is.

"A great idea is not enough."

— Rosabeth Moss Kanter (Kanter, n.d.)

What is innovation?

Defining innovation is "one of the biggest challenges of innovation" (Welsh, 2018). Even in the writing of this book, our team of authors had great debate. In an oversimplified way, innovation is simply the introduction of something new or different that adds value. Definitions range from simple to complex. Healthcare innovation can be defined as:

The adoption of those best-demonstrated practices that have been proven to be successful and implementation of those practices while ensuring the safety and best outcomes for patients and whose adoption might also affect the performance of the organization. In other words, innovation in healthcare is defined as "those changes that help healthcare practitioners focus on the patient by helping healthcare professionals work smarter, faster, better, and more cost effectively" (Thakkur, Hsu & Fontenot, 2012, p. 364).

Another definition is that "an innovation is a new way of doing things to improve health care delivery. An innovation may be a product, a service, a process, a system, an organizational structure, or a business model. If it is new to your organization, it is an innovation, even if it has been around for a while in other contexts" (Amoosegar, Brach, Lenfestey, Roussel, Sorens, 2008, p.5). However, in order for the adoption of innovation to occur, the innovations must prove practical and produce a better outcome and/or efficiency than the current state. A personal definition based on experience working with accelerators, academics, and other startup entrepreneurs is that "innovation is the introduction of something new, using systems and documented processes, while exercising resource management, to create something, accepted into a market, due to a perceived value" (Nix, 2018).

Innovation is not just about developing new technologies, gizmos, gadgets, or devices. It is about new models of care, new practices or processes. It can even be social innovation to reduce health disparities and improve health equity or reduce the impacts of social determinants of health by mitigating the negative impact and addressing big social challenges, such as homelessness, food insecurity, and social isolation. So often, people think of innovation as being cool tech stuff.

Examples of innovations in healthcare:

- innovative programs to promote breastfeeding in vulnerable infants

- innovations in quality improvement (e.g., improved patient outcomes as a measure of payment)

- innovative solutions to address healthcare quality (e.g., urinary catheter protocol)

- innovative approaches to quality improvement projects on a unit-wide scale (e.g., elevating HOB to decrease VAP)

- innovative changes to drive healthcare savings (e.g., nurse fellowship program for on-the-job training)

- advancing health policy (e.g., engaging nursing students in health policy work)

- innovation in health information technology (e.g., development of barcode medication administration)

- simulation training (e.g., simulation experiences in nursing education)

- innovations in delegation skills (e.g., simulation experiences)

(Thomas, Siefert, & Joyner, 2016, p. 3)

The multiple definitions and examples can be confusing, and there are a multitude of processes, theories, and systems to guide innovation. There is often fear of innovation due to the need for change and consistent decision making. Advancing innovation requires information or data, which may often be insufficient. Decision making while on the innovation journey occurs no matter how sound the data, often requiring best guesses based on what is known at the time. Doesn't that sound like nursing, where we navigate the waters to the best of our ability by using experts and collaboration through cross-functional teams to help us and our patients on their journey? No matter the industry, innovation is being hailed as the key to its relevance and transformation. To yield competitive advantage, it is essential to create products and processes that others desire and utilize, as this results in better outcomes and a better financial return.

Innovation affords opportunity to grow. However, innovation is a risk and is often mitigated and even carefully monitored in healthcare. Due to the fact that patients and their families entrust us with their care, we must first "do no harm." In order to continue to grow and thrive, our industry must look to develop an appetite for risk. Risk-taking is engaging in a behavior that involves risk in order to achieve a goal (Cianelli, Clipper, Freeman, Goldstein, & Wyatt, 2016). We know that "[i]n the healthcare industry, risk often is viewed as a negative term and risk-taking behavior is strongly discouraged and avoided" (Cianelli, et al., 2016, pg. 7).

In order to implement the systems and processes that allow healthcare to innovate from within, we can learn from industries already accelerating in innovation and changing our lives daily. One such example is Amazon, which has grown from its initial offering of books to become a retail powerhouse. Part of their growth is attributed to the internal process that empowers every employee to build the "next best thing" through a process called "working backward." At Amazon, the process of "working backward" starts with a document written by the employee with the idea. These documents are then presented to the employee's leader to determine if they or any other leader is willing to put resources behind it (Vogels, 2006, para.1).

According to Vogels (2006), the "Working Backward" product definition process is about fleshing out the concept and achieving clarity of thought about what we will ultimately go off and build. It typically has four steps:

1. **Start by writing the press release**. The press release describes in a simple way what the product does and why it exists—what its features and benefits are. It needs to be very clear and to the point. Writing a press release up front clarifies how the world will see the product.

2. **Write a frequently asked questions document**. This contains questions that came up when we wrote the press release. Include questions that were asked when the press release was shared, as well as questions that define what the product is good for. Put yourself in the shoes of someone using the product, and consider all queries that might arise.

3. **Define the customer experience**. Describe in precise detail the customer experience for the different things that a customer might do with the product. For products with a user interface, build mockups of each screen that the customer uses. For web services, write use cases, including code snippets, that describe ways people will use the product. The goal here is to tell stories of how a customer is solving their problems using the product.

4. **Write the user manual**. The user manual is what a customer will use to find out about the product and how to use it. The user manual typically has three sections: concepts, how-to, and references. These tell the customer everything they need to know to use the product.

"Once we have gone through the process of creating the press release, frequently asked questions, mockups, and user manuals, it is amazing how much clearer it is what we are planning to build. We'll have a suite of documents that we can use to explain the new product to other teams within Amazon. At that point, we know that the whole team has a shared vision on the product we are going to build" (Vogels, 2006, para. 4-7).

Skill-building exercise

Take your idea/innovation and work backward. Start by writing your own press release, write a set of frequently asked questions, define your customer experience, and finally, draft the user manual for your idea/innovation. When complete, see if your idea still makes sense.

"Do no harm, but take no s***."

— Gavin Nascimento (Nascimento, 2016)

Why not consider innovation?

A question worth asking is, why not consider innovation? What would happen if you decided not to work toward innovation? Things would likely remain the same. However, generally speaking, everything is constantly changing, even if only incrementally. Not pursuing innovation is the choice to continue to allow change to occur *to* you versus *with* you or *by* you. When not driving toward innovation, you decrease your personal leverage by giving up power, relevance, or your seat at the table. Shifting the power differential this way even diminishes the value you bring as a nurse. Our advice: don't give this up! No matter what institution or organization we work for, it is the nurse who is in the prime position to know the answers to many questions that families, physicians, medical students, sales representatives, and many more are actively seeking. In fact, somebody is most likely looking for you right now to answer one of their questions. You might wonder that if nurses have this much knowledge, why are we not leading the innovation and change that is necessary to transform health? Great question. This topic will be discussed later in this book.

Call to action

> As you read this book, be sure to write down your ideas, take notes, use tabs, "dogear" pages, and make highlights. Use this as a your project guide so that by the time you have finished reading, you will have notes to help with your business plan, marketing plan, sales strategy, and product launch. Or use this book at a tool to help you solve challenges within your organization or develop new models of care. Start with your idea, and follow it through each chapter, fine-tuning your idea from start to finish.

Networking

The importance of effective networking should not be understated; it will make advancing your work exponentially more successful. It is valuable to attend "meetups" (e.g., Meetup.com) on topics of interest. To increase the size and scope of your network, always be sure to distribute and collect business cards, which is the "old school" way, or swap LinkedIn profiles (at LinkedIn.com) to connect in the future. It is smart to build your network so you can access assistance, resources, potential funders, coaches, mentors,and support as necessary. Be sure to thank people who help you, and reach out every couple of months to keep your network alive for those whom either you can help or who may someday help you. Take opportunities to pay it forward when you can as well. Help others whom you may be a step ahead of. A good network is a powerful resource to have access to.

We are not legal or finance experts; we are all nurses with experience as inventors, innovators, and entreprenurses. Be sure to consult an accountant and an attorney if you are serious about advancing your work, because this book is not a substitute for legal or financial advice. We will share our journeys, stories, and lessons learned to inspire and provoke you into thought and action to advance your own work. Our goal is to see nurses lead innovation in healthcare. This book gives you the permission to stop looking for others *to* build change and to start looking for others to build change *with*. Focus on "leaning in" to the power that you have and helping to shift power to other frontline caregivers/nurses. Work to be the change, to initiate the innovation, and to "get shift done."

References

Amoosegar, J., Brach, C., Lenfestey, N., & Roussel, A., & Sorens, A. (2008). Will it work here? A decision-maker's guide to adopting innovations. Rockville, MD: Agency for Healthcare Research and Quality. Accessed on February 23, 2019. Accessed from https://innovations.ahrq.gov/sites/default/files/guides/InnovationAdoptionGuide.pdf.

Burton, N. (2017). Our Hierarchy of Needs. Psychology Today. Accessed on March 13, 2019. Accessed from https://www.psychologytoday.com/us/blog/hide-and-seek/201205/our-hierarchy-needs.

Cianelli, R., Clipper, B., Freeman, R., Goldstein, J. & Wyatt, T. (2016). *The Innovation Road Map: A Guide for Nurse Leaders*. Greensboro, NC. Published by Innovation Works.

Gary, J. (2012). The Use of Positive Deviance to Deliver Patient-Centered Care (Doctoral Dissertation). Accessed from Scholar Works at UT Tyler, https://scholarworks.uttyler.edu/nursing_grad/28/. Accessed on March 4, 2019.

Johansson, F. (2006). *The Medici effect : what elephants and epidemics can teach us about innovation*. Boston, Massachusetts. Harvard Business School Press.

Kanter, R. (n.d.). Rosabeth Moss Kanter Quotes. Accessed on March 4, 2019. Accessed from BrainyQuote.com https://www.brainyquote.com/quotes/rosabeth_moss_kanter_380594.

Kumar D. (2012, July 18) *Components of Creativity*. Accessed on March 4, 2019. Accessed from https://kumardeepak.wordpress.com/2012/07/18/components-of-creativity/

Kurtz, G. & Kershner, I. (1980) *The Empire Strikes Back* [Motion Picture]. USA: Twentieth Century Fox Corporation: Lucasfilm, ltd.

Merriam-Webster Dictionary. (n.d.). Idea. Accessed on February 19, 2019. Accessed from https://www.merriam- webster.com/dictionary/idea.

Merriam-Webster. (n.d.). Invention. Accessed on February 19, 2019. Accessed from https://www.merriam- webster.com/dictionary/invention.

Nakamura, J., & Csikszentmihalyi, M. (2015). The Motivational Sources of Creativity as Viewed from the Paradigm of Positive Psychology. (pp. 195-206). *The Systems Model of Creativity: The Collected Works of Mihaly Csikszentmihalyi* .Geneva, Switzerland. Springer Press.

Nascimento, G, (2016, November 15). *Do no harm but take no s...; a simple philosophy.* Accessed on March 4, 2019. Accessed from https://anewkindofhuman.com/no-harm-take-no-shit/.

Nix, W. (2018, October 19). Personal communication, From Problem to Solution: Inspiring Nurses to innovate. *6th Annual Nursing Innovation Summit.* Accessed on March 4, 2019. Accessed from https://www.youtube.com/watch?v=I1-v0Jib24g&t=536s.

Rumi (n.d.) Accessed on March 4, 2019. Accessed from https://en.wikiquote.org/wiki/Rumi.

Sinek, S. (September 7, 2012). "Dream big. Start small. But most of all, start.". Accessed on March 4, 2019. Accessed from Twitter.

Thakkur, R., Hsu, S., & Fontenot, G. (2012) Innovation in healthcare: Issues and Future Trends. Journal of Business Research. 65 (pp.562-569).

Thomas, T., Seifert, P., & Joyner, J., (September 30, 2016). Registered Nurses Leading Innovative Changes. The Online Journal of Issues in Nursing. 21(3). Manuscript 3. Accessed on March 4, 2019. Accessed from http://ojin.nursingworld.org/MainMenuCategories/ANAMarketplace/AN-APeriodicals/OJIN/TableofContents/Vol-21-2016/No3-Sept-2016/Registered-Nurses-Leading-Innovative-Changes.html.

Welsh, M. (2018, November 12). Nurses Leading Innovation. (Blog post). Accessed on March 4, 2019. Accessed from https://nursing.jnj.com/nurse-innovator-entrepreneur-emphasizes-adding-value-to-patient-care?fbclid=IwAR1n9iI0mR_ByoC6sSZfMZOfDwgRYUaCqr1Jjqcwb-UOu9_ehVIM-0kPiRa0.

Vogels, W. (2006). Working Backwards (blog entry). Accessed on March 4, 2019. Accessed from https://www.allthingsdistributed.com/2006/11/working_backwards.html.

2

Developing an Innovator's Mindset

By Dr. Brian Weirich

Objectives

By the end of this chapter, the reader will be able to:

- Explain the mindset needed to increase your pathway to success.

- Describe common pitfalls and reasons for innovation failure.

- Identify practices and habits to overcome innovation adversity.

> *"Deep down I was searching for something else, something more. I had an aching sense that our time is short, shorter than we ever know, short as a morning run, and I wanted mine to be meaningful. And purposeful. And creative. And important. Above all . . . different. I wanted to leave a mark on the world."* —Phil Knight, NIKE Founder (Knight, 2016, p. 3)

In wilderness survival, there's an analogy often used to describe great adventures, which states that most people go about their lives like a fish in a tank. It's safe. Oxygen and food are readily available, and you see the same fish every day and have a generally predictable routine. Now take those fish and place them in a lake. The world is now foreign, a treacherous path ahead as the search begins for those basic needs as described by Maslow. There are also great rewards that can be earned by those who keep going, those who take calculated risks and learn from mistakes. This analogy also applies to entrepreneurship, especially nurse entrepreneurs.

Nurses are not taught the entrepreneur basics in school—there are no business basics, innovation, or design thinking clinicals in addition to our medical-surgical, home care, and behavioral health rotations. As we enter the workforce, the clinical setting we were prepared for becomes predictably monotonous with twelve-hour shifts, staff meetings, new hire orientation/mentoring, and policy/ practice changes that come and go frequently. By this time, perhaps your purpose has changed. Maybe you're unhappy with the status quo or you have a great product, care model, or idea that can change or even fix a dysfunctional and ineffective healthcare system. Where does a nurse go from here?

In the face of uncertainty, our first instinct is often to reject novelty—we look for reasons that unfamiliar concepts might fail. These may also be known as "originals." We've all heard the statistic that nine out of ten businesses fail. We've seen *Shark Tank*, where the Sharks laugh at the entrepreneur's ideas, prototypes, and valuations and say, "You have a hobby, not a business." Then there are those entrepreneurs who have invested hundreds of thousands of dollars and still have little to no revenue to show for it. It is important to know that rejection is part of the journey, so why would someone leave their safety net and choose this path? Are you sure you want to?

> *"When everything seems to be going against you, remember the airplane takes off against the wind, not with it."*
>
> *— Henry Ford, founder of Ford Motors (McCulleyconsulting.com, 2018)*

Mindset

In 2011, co-founders Steven Krein and Unity Stoakes got together to build what they referred to as a global army, focused on a shared common goal: transforming healthcare. As a result, they created StartUp Health, a New York-based coaching program and peer network for healthcare entrepreneurs. They introduced a revolutionary new model for transforming health by organizing, supporting, and investing in a global army of entrepreneurs called Health Transformers. StartUp Health™ invests in ten Health "Moonshots" to improve the health and wellbeing of everyone in the world.

The goal of StartUp Health is to invest and partner with 1,000 digital healthcare tech companies. To accomplish this, they are constantly vetting (assessing) startups that can disrupt healthcare on a wide spectrum of variables. However, one attribute of successful startups stands out as a non-negotiable: the mindset of the founders. How dedicated are the founders, really? What's their motivation? How will they respond when faced with adversity and setbacks? To answer these questions, they have created a mindset scorecard that they require companies to frequently use for self-assessments.

Although there are many mindsets, StartUp Health chooses to focus on eight critical mindsets, using these to help innovators identify where they mentally are at any given time during their journey. Below is a look at StartUp Health's *MINDSET SCORECARD* (StartUphealth.com, 2019):

THE HEALTH TRANSFORMER MINDSET SCORECARD™   STARTUP +HEALTH

Mindsets	1 2 3	4 5 6	7 8 9	10 11 12 A B
1 Long-term Commitment	You are not "all in" yet and not fully ready to commit your life to transforming health.	You are working on other things until you have more certainty that you're on the right path to transforming health.	You are fully committed but don't have clear vision beyond the next 12-24 months on how you'll transform health.	You are "all in" and will do whatever it takes for as long as it takes, because it is your life's mission to transform health.
2 Supportive Relationships	You don't feel like you can rely on others, would rather do everything yourself and have no long-term relationships on your team.	You "kind of" have a team and spend too much of your time convincing or reminding people around you of your vision.	You have a great team but still feel lonely and like no one quite understands why you always want and push for more.	You are continually surrounded by like-minded people who support, encourage, and believe in you and your vision.
3 Quarterly & Weekly Rhythm	You are heads down and don't feel the need to step back, celebrate wins or recalibrate to figure out "what's working/not working."	You constantly feel like you haven't accomplished "enough" so you try to catch up over weekends, with each week and month blending into the next.	You intuitively know what you need to do each week and quarter but Fridays arrive and quarters end without you achieving what you planned.	You recalibrate every 90 days, begin each week with a written plan and end each period celebrating the iterations and progress you made by sharing with your Backable Team.
4 Confidently Ambitious	You have an interesting idea but given everyone's skepticism you aren't 100% sure if it's a good idea.	You haven't "sold yourself 100% on achieving your vision and people can see that you're feeling beat up by daily challenges.	You keep hearing reasons why your idea won't succeed, so you keep making your plans more "realistic" and less transformative.	You always convey confidence and an ambitious vision for transforming health, regardless of how many times you get knocked down.
5 Self Aware	You talk more than you listen and aren't able to clearly articulate what your unique ability is.	You are working really hard, doing things that you hate doing and aren't really good at but "someone" has to do it.	You know what your "unique ability" is but are not really leveraging other people's unique abilities often enough to amplify your efforts.	You are coachable and self-aware of your unique abilities, and the unique abilities of others, so you continually improve your capabilities and results.
6 Healthy Habits	You don't feel the need to take care of yourself because that's just the life of an entrepreneur.	You know you need to take better care of yourself but don't have the time, which negatively impacts your valuable relationships.	You make time for your family and yourself but occasionally slip into old habits when work gets too busy.	You take care of yourself, have a clear mind and healthy body, and regularly practice gratitude, both to yourself and with others.
7 Value Creator	You are increasingly worried that other people are going to cheat you in business and life.	You know how to create value for yourself and others but are continually frustrated by lack of progress and current resources.	You find yourself continually relying on past accomplishments to justify your value creation potential.	You are continually making your future bigger than your past, attracting and developing new capabilities and resources.
8 Batteries Included	You find yourself in frequent non-constructive arguments with your team and advisors, draining your energy and the energy of those around you.	You are often told you give energy to those around you, but constantly feel your interactions with others drains your energy.	You provide energy to those closest to you, but have not eliminated people from your life and business that drain your energy.	You are always providing energy to others and have no tolerance for those who drain energy so you fill your life with "batteries included" people.
	UNCOMMITTED ENTREPRENEUR	FRUSTRATED ENTREPRENEUR	HEALTH ENTREPRENEUR	HEALTH TRANSFORMER

Skill-building exercise:

Using the StartUp Health mindset scorecard and grading rubric, evaluate your current mindset.

MINDSET		
Long-Term Commitment	1 2 3 4 5 6 7 8 9 10 11 12	
Supportive Relationship	1 2 3 4 5 6 7 8 9 10 11 12	
Quarterly & Weekly Rhythm	1 2 3 4 5 6 7 8 9 10 11 12	
Confidently Ambitious	1 2 3 4 5 6 7 8 9 10 11 12	
Self-Aware	1 2 3 4 5 6 7 8 9 10 11 12	
Healthy Habits	1 2 3 4 5 6 7 8 9 10 11 12	
Value Creator	1 2 3 4 5 6 7 8 9 10 11 12	
Batteries Included	1 2 3 4 5 6 7 8 9 10 11 12	
TOTAL SCORE	Write score here	Failure (<24) Frustrated (24-48) Conventional (49-72) Transformative (73-96)

(With permission. StartUphealth.com, 2019)

Motivational speaker Les Brown says, "Draw your line in the sand. Make your decision now and start taking action to living your dream. By not taking bold steps to live your dream, not only are you missing out on fully living, but the world is missing out on the greatness you have to offer. Be bold" (2015). The world of entrepreneurship is not easy. It will take a significant level of commitment, resilience, and risk taking. There will be many ups and downs, good days followed by bad days, which will be followed by worse days. In order to move forward in this fast-paced environment, one has to commit to the task at hand, knowing there will be pitfalls ahead that only you can get yourself past. You first have to make this commitment. You have to draw the line in the sand and commit 100 percent.

Do you have an innovator's mindset? Have you drawn a line in the sand? If the answer to those two questions is yes, then you're on the right track, so keep going but know that the path doesn't get easier. On the contrary, it's an unpredictable world that will repeatedly test your ambition, mindset, commitment, and desire to succeed. It's inevitable that sometime in the future, you'll find yourself in what is known as the trough of sorrow.

The Trough of Sorrow

Life as an innovator is not easy. Rather, it is filled with a ton of uncertainty, unexpected challenges, and a pressure to succeed. There is a mental struggle that comes with getting momentum for your idea. Paul Graham, cofounder of Y Combinator, developed a term for that struggle: the Trough of Sorrow. This refers to the period of struggle that a startup faces after a setback. Following the initial excitement of starting a company is the challenge to find product-market fit, which requires significant amounts of determination and perseverance. Paul Graham also created the Startup Curve, which depicts the process and the Trough of Sorrow (Graham 2019):

The Trough of Sorrow is so prevalent because the path to success is not straight and does not grow as planned from the beginning, like popular depictions may have us believe. Getting through the challenges following the initial excitement is extremely difficult. When you're consistently one month away from failure, it can wreak havoc on anyone's mental health. The fact is, depression, anxiety, and extreme levels of stress run rampant in the startup community. But until recently, no one has talked about it. As a result, entrepreneurs often feel alone in their responsibility to make their company succeed, which makes the Trough of Sorrow even more difficult to endure.

One entrepreneur described her own experience in the Trough of Sorrow. She mentions various levels of sorrow, the first being Limbo. Limbo is where you are most of the time when you start a company. You're working insane hours, you never think of anything but your enterprise, and you still have no idea if anything good will come of it. You also don't have any money because you're putting everything back into the company and not paying yourself a living wage (Bounde, 2015).

the startup curve

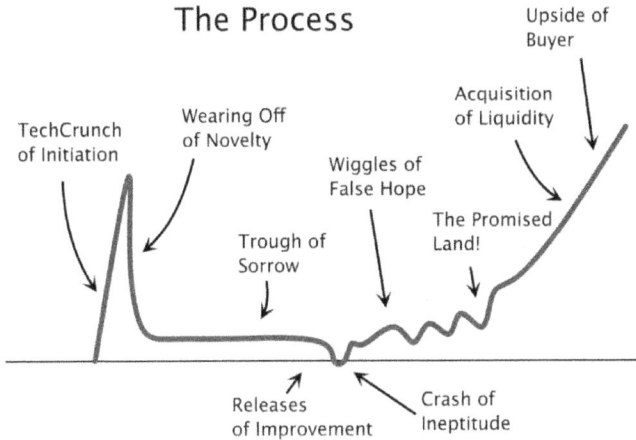

The Process

Upside of Buyer

Acquisition of Liquidity

TechCrunch of Initiation

Wearing Off of Novelty

Wiggles of False Hope

The Promised Land!

Trough of Sorrow

Releases of Improvement

Crash of Ineptitude

(With permission. Graham, 2019)

The entrepreneur world also refers to this phase of ambiguity as "bootstrapping." The bottom of the Trough is where you doubt your very sanity: "How could I have been this wrong? Where were my mentors?" This is when you know every decision you have ever made was wrong. It's when you lie on the living room floor and go through each point of your life and realize that you should have made the other choice (Rits, 2015). When you drew the line in the sand, you left your safety net. Now what?

The fortunate thing about the Trough of Sorrow is that every entrepreneur has been there, even the best. There are great case studies about the founders of Airbnb living in the trough, always a few days away from insolvency and on the verge of a complete pivot or collapse. Now, they are a "unicorn" (a startup worth $1B market value) company that has transformed an industry forever.

How can we learn from Airbnb and others who have successfully risen out of the Trough and onto success? What could you, the innovator, be doing now to prepare for these dreadful days that make you question the very purpose you've come to identify with?

"It isn't enough to think outside the box. Thinking is passive. Get used to acting outside the box." —Tim Ferriss, podcaster, author, entrepreneur (Moore, 2018)

Develop habits of success

Journaling

What do John D. Rockefeller, Thomas Edison, Ernest Hemingway, Henry David Thoreau, Kurt Cobain, Christopher Columbus, and Ronald Reagan all have in common? Other than all having influenced and shaped our world in some way, they were all regular journalers.

People often think of journaling as synonymous with keeping a diary, and thoughts of angry tweens writing words of rebellion against parents come to mind. This is not the case. Journaling zones in your reactions, perceptions, and feelings to events, with the hopes of gaining clarity and making positive changes when and wherever necessary. It's also a good problem-solving tool; often, one can hash out a problem and come up with solutions more easily on paper.

Other benefits include:

- Gaining Clarity: Journaling offers a glimpse into your working mind.

- Building Empathy: When you start to look at things objectively, you can better understand other points of view.

- Feeling Calmer: Have you ever written an angry letter/email and never sent it? How did that make you feel? Journaling is a bit like that.

- Solving Problems: Sometimes the only way to arrive at the answer of a complex problem is to tap into the creative, intuitive, and emotional right brain, which is what journaling does.

- Tracking Patterns: Many doctors advise their patients to track physical symptoms to gauge their progress. Similarly, journaling serves as a kind of mental tracker.

Also, consider gratitude journaling, which is a more contemporary way of journaling that has become popular recently. Gratitude is a way for people to appreciate what they have instead of always reaching for something new in the hopes it will make them happier or thinking they can't feel satisfied until every physical and material need is met. Gratitude helps people refocus on what they have instead of what they lack. Although it may feel contrived at first, this mental state grows stronger with use and practice (Harvard Mental Health, 2011). There are currently a variety of templates online or mobile apps that offer infrastructure and motivation to stay on top of the practice of gratitude.

Reading

Reading daily has many benefits on a person's physical and emotional well-being. According to Health Fitness Revolution (2015), there are many more benefits than what we typically think of, such as:

- **Stimulating the mind:** Keeping your brain active and engaged prevents it from losing its power by sharpening its logical ability.

- **Acquiring knowledge:** Everything you read fills your head with new bits of information, and you never know when it might come in handy. The more knowledge you have, the better equipped you are to tackle challenges ahead.

- **Expanding vocabulary:** The more you read, the more words you are exposed to. These words will inevitably make their way into your everyday vocabulary, which will help significantly as your peer group and circle of influence in the innovation space becomes different than those you previously associated with.

- **Sharpening critical and analytical skills:** You've just entered a new world with new experiences and obstacles. Your previous career and milestones may not have prepared you emotionally and physically for what you will face ahead. You will become more dependent on your critical thinking and analytical skills for survival.

- **Improving memory:** Every new memory you create forges new synapses and strengthens existing ones, which assists in short-term memory recall.

- **Boosting concentration:** Reading allows you to remove the noise and distraction from social media and immerse yourself in every fine detail seen from the point of view of another.

- **Feeding your imagination:** In the world of innovation, you're attempting to solve a problem in a way that doesn't currently exist. A wild imagination may be your best asset. The story of a book will absorb your mind, so let your imagination fly. While you are reading, you are building images, faces, places, colors, settings, and stimulating your creative juices.

- **Reducing stress:** No matter how much stress you are going through, reading a good story can help take your mind off these difficult situations. A good novel can distract you, while an interesting article can slip your mind out of your problems at the present moment.

Many of the most successful people credit reading in some capacity to their success. Let's look at the reading habits of highly successful people as strong examples (Weller, 2017).

Oprah Winfrey: Since 1996, the veteran talk-show host has been advising her viewers' reading habits with Oprah's Book Club. Winfrey has called reading "her personal path to freedom" (Weller, 2017, para. 13).

Warren Buffett: The Berkshire Hathaway magnate reportedly spends five to six hours a day reading five different newspapers. He also combs through 500 pages of financial documents and recommends prospective investors do the same.

Bill Gates: The former Microsoft CEO has attested to reading fifty books a year, or roughly one book a week. Most of the books are non-fiction, dealing with public health, disease, engineering, business, and science.

Mark Zuckerberg: In 2015, the Facebook CEO vowed to read one book every other week, "with an emphasis on learning about different cultures, beliefs, histories and technologies," as he wrote in a Facebook post. "Books allow you to fully explore a topic and immerse yourself in a deeper way than most media today. I'm looking forward to shifting more of my media diet towards reading books" (Weller, 2017, para.11).

Mark Cuban: Dallas Mavericks owner Mark Cuban is a vocal supporter of treating business like a sport, which means he looks for the competitive edge however he can. Often, that means reading for three hours every day just to learn more about the industries he works in. Cuban has said this worked wonders at the start of his career. "Everything I read was public," he wrote in his blog's Success and Motivation series. "Anyone could buy the same books and magazines. The same information was available to anyone who wanted it. Turns out most people didn't want it" (Weller, 2017, para 16).

Elon Musk: Long before he became the CEO of Tesla and even before he co-founded PayPal, a young Elon Musk was reading science-fiction novels for up to ten hours a day. He also reportedly read through the entire *Encyclopedia Britannica* when he was nine years old. He still credits a love of books for his vast knowledge about rockets. When asked how he knew so much about them, he said, "I read a lot of books" (Weller, 2017, para. 25).

 (Weller, 2017)

Reading helps you learn from both the mistakes and successes of others. Instead of just diving in, relying on instinct and motivation to lead you, reading provides a mental map to bypass rookie mistakes people make on the innovation journey, as well as life in general. You will undoubtedly make mistakes along your innovation journey. Reading will re-center you, keep you up to date on your market, and provide guardrails for your dreams and ideas to advance.

Call to action

Research and compile a reading list from online or book sources. Consider Success.com, Medium.com, Audible.com, Blinkist.com, *Entrepreneur*, *INC* magazine, etc. Build a LinkedIn profile and follow industry leaders, such as our team of authors, as well as others. Prioritize your reading list so you spend time every day or every other day reading something of value that will help you advance your innovation, ideas, and invention and/or to improve yourself.

Exercise/Fitness:

Successful business moguls like Mark Wahlberg and Richard Branson credit exercise as an important ritual that is a top priority as they plan their day. Even while in the White House, holding the highest position in the world, President Obama made running outside a priority. Although not professional athletes, all claim exercise was an important habit that had a direct correlation to their success. Here are a few reasons that innovators should make exercise a habit:

It triggers the primal regions of the brain and psyche: Physiologically, outdoor exercise has been shown to inspire a greater commitment to an exercise program. Through this, you trigger the more primal regions of your brain and psyche. Exercising outdoors increases mental and emotional well-being by way of increased energy, regeneration, positivity, gratification, satisfaction, pleasure, self-esteem, liveliness, passion, and a sense of accomplishment (Campbell, 2016).

It builds your brain and helps break bad habits: After a long day of work, it's tempting to crash in front of the TV and eat or drink your frustrations away. You worked hard and you may think you deserve it. That's one of the best things about exercise: it puts your mind in contact with your body and makes them whole. Taking those few minutes out of your day to workout lets you do a rundown on what you really need and allows you to collect your thoughts and instill a sense of direction instead of letting you indulge yourself. It's really the best way to break any destructive habits that stand in your way (Cohen, 2016).

It puts you in a positive mood: Raising your heart rate is revitalizing. It clears your mind of wasteful thoughts and emotions and allows you to put stress to the side as you focus on being in the zone (Campbell, 2016).

It builds self-esteem for a healthier you: Exercise not only decreases stress but also teaches you that you can excel beyond the limitations you've set for yourself. It builds your body and mind into a sharper tool, and knowing and feeling that does wonders for your self-esteem (Cohen, 2016).

You'll work smarter, not harder: We know corporate retreats are a great way to increase morale and team build. Unfortunately, these tend to be difficult to put together and happen infrequently. However, a pickup basketball game or company baseball game can be done fairly easily and lead to similar results. Plus, unlike some retreats, they are a great and fun way to exercise and light the fire in your belly! Having a regular commitment outside the office can be incredibly necessary. Just as you can burn out from over-exercise, you can hit a point of diminishing returns if you stay much longer than eight hours at the office. Scheduled or spontaneous workout time can help you make the most of your work time by keeping you aware that when it's quitting time, it's really quitting time. And it's comforting to know that even if you're not at work, you're building a more focused, more productive you. Doing it with coworkers has the added benefit of bringing everyone together and maybe even solving a few problems on the court!

It is often publicized that many of the Fortune 500 and other innovative companies in the world, including Google, Apple, and even Deloitte, have onsite exercise facilities. The reason is simple: making exercise easily accessible eliminates an excuse and encourages staff to use the facilities. In turn, this exercise makes everyone at the company sharper and more competitive and therefore, makes the company itself sharper and more competitive. Even "old world" companies like big banks and accounting firms are building exercise rooms into their new facilities because they know it leads to better results.

Work can be frustrating. You may be pushing yourself to do the best you can, but whether it's negative supervisors, gossipy coworkers, or just feeling stuck doing the same thing over and over again, it can be difficult to stay engaged at work when this feeling strikes. If you fall victim to this thinking, your career will suffer, so you'll need to shake it up and find a way to relieve the stress. Regular exercise not only keeps you in the fight but also gets you working harder, better, and smarter.

After all, if you want to be the best, you have to be your best self. So, keep pushing yourself to climb and compete, both physically and mentally. As you do, you'll see that the negative voices have less power. The naysayers will fall to the wayside as you regain control of your mood, your body, your career, and your life. Don't accept limitations. Keep working, and don't give up—especially not on yourself (Cohen, 2016).

> *"The great danger for most of us lies not in setting our aim too high and falling short; but in setting our aim too low, and achieving our mark."*
>
> —Michelangelo *(Mayberry, 2017)*

Take time to appreciate accomplishments

As you go through the constant rollercoaster of innovation and entrepreneurship, it's easy to visualize the end goal. This picture came to mind when you creatively solved a problem and began down this path. In order to get to where you want to go, you must have progress markers along the way to ensure that you are heading in the right direction, that you're still on target and to show progress when it feels like an impossible uphill battle.

Many use the SMART goal setting technique to make it easier to set goals that you will accomplish.

SMART stands for:

- *Specific* — Keep goals clear, concise, and simple.
- *Measurable* — Define action plans to measure.
- *Achievable* — Keep goals incremental.
- *Realistic* — Match goals to needs and ambitions.
- *Timetable* — Add milestones and completion dates.

   (Whitaker, 2015)

All big accomplishments are completed by meeting smaller milestones along the way. Reflect often, and constantly set and evaluate your current mindset, commitment, and traction on short- and long-term goals. Plan carefully how you can create a routine for excellence. Spend the time and effort to cultivate an innovator's mindset, and success is closer than you think.

   Authors' Note: The quotes from this chapter come from a variety of source types. Not all are associated with a corresponding page number.

References

Bounde. (2015, October 6). What is the trough of sorrow, anyway? Retrieved on March 14, 2019. Retrieved from https://medium.com/@BoundeHQ/what-is-the-trough-of-sorrow-anyway-d81c32023668.

Brown, L. (2015, December 6). @thelesbrown. Retrieved on March 17, 2019. Retrieved from from https://www.facebook.com/thelesbrown/posts/10153705706839654.

Campbell, S. (2016, April 14). Retrieved on March 9, 2019. Retrieved from https://www.entrepreneur.com/article/273995.

Cohen, J. (2016, June 6). Exercise is one thing most successful people do everyday. Retrieved on March 14, 2019. Retrieved from https://www.entrepreneur.com/article/276760.

Graham, P. (2019). The startup curve. Retrieved on March 14, 2019. Retrieved from https://www.bing.com/images/search?q=paul+graham+startup+curve&FORM=HDRSC2.

Harvard Mental Health Letter. (2011, November). In praise of gratitude. Harvard Health Publishing: Harvard Medical School. Retrieved on March 14, 2019. Retrieved from https://www.health.harvard.edu/newsletter_article/in-praise-of-gratitude.

Health Fitness Revolution. (2015, May 15). Top 10 health benefits of reading. Retrieved on March 14, 2019. Retrieved from http://www.healthfitnessrevolution.com/top-10-healthbenefits-reading/.

Healthmatters.idaho.gov. (2018, July). Health Matters [Image]. Retrieved on March 17, 2019. Retrieved from https://healthmatters.idaho.gov/pdf/POSTERS/AIRPLANE_POSTER_July2018.pdf.

Knight, P. (2016). Shoe dog. New York, NY: Simon & Schuster.

Mayberry, M. (2017, January 18). 10 great quotes on the power of goals. Entrepreneur. Retrieved on March 17, 2019. Retrieved from https://www.entrepreneur.com/article/287411.

McCulleyconsulting.com. (2018). Henry Ford quote. Retrieved on March 18, 2019. Retrieved from https://www.mcculleyconsulting.com/inspiring-quotes.

Moore, J. I. (2018). 40 Tim Ferriss quotes from 4 hour workweek and tools of titans. *Everyday Power*. Retrieved on March 17, 2019. Retrieved from https://everydaypowerblog.com/tim-ferriss-quotes/.

Rits, S. (2015). The trough of sorrows and how to climb out. Project Eve: Reinvent your Career. Retrieved on February 14, 2019. Retrieved from https://projecteve.com/the-trough-of-sorrows-and-how-to-climbout/.

StartUp Health. (2019). Mindset scorecard. Retrieved on March 11, 2019. Retrieved from https://www.startuphealth.com/.

Weller, C. (2017, July 20). 9 of the most successful people share their reading habits. Business Insider. Retrieved on February 14, 2019. Retrieved from https://www.businessinsider.com/what-successful-people-read-2017-7.

Whitaker, R. (2015, December 29). Harvard study: Smart goals and you. About Leaders. Retrieved on March 14, 2019. Retrieved from https://aboutleaders.com/harvard-study-smart-goals-and-you/#gs.1io6l1.

3 Entrepreneurship

By Rebecca Love

Objectives

By the end of this chapter, the reader will be able to:

- Explain the difference between entrepreneurship vs. intrapreneurship.
- Articulate pitfalls of an entrepreneur and how they can be avoided.
- Describe how the small business association can help you launch a new business.
- Identify how innovation is the foundation of entrepreneurship.

  "All our dreams can come true, if we have the courage to pursue them".

  — Walt Disney (Bigcommerce.com, 2019)

From when I was a little girl to well after college, I never dreamed about being an entrepreneur. I'm not sure if that is unique to me or if other nurse entrepreneurs felt this way as well. I had never been exposed to the concept of entrepreneurship or innovation in nursing school. I was not aware that our drive and desire as nurses to alleviate suffering and help others is actually a fundamental principle of entrepreneurship. In fact, most entrepreneurs become entrepreneurs because they have a desire to make something better; it becomes a passion to solve challenges, and fundamentally, this is exactly what we do as nurses.

When I decided to become a nurse, I dreamed of making people's lives better, caring for patients, and doing good in the world. What I didn't know is that one day, being confronted by a challenge that had no solution, I would literally lie awake in bed in the middle of the night, feeling more passionately than I ever had in my life that I needed to do something about it on a large scale. It was there that my journey in entrepreneurship began.

I now tell my story in front of nurses and even on TEDx Talks. My start on this journey may be similar to your own—entrepreneurs are often more similar than people realize. You may feel lost in your journey of entrepreneurship but passionate about creating a solution, just as I did when I started out.

My personal journey started in March 2013, when I was a hospice nurse practitioner. At that time, a patient whom I was visiting one morning was told that her family was moving her to a nursing home because they couldn't find affordable care to keep her at home, and she was devastated. I left this visit feeling deflated and headed back to my community college office, where I worked as professor of nursing. When I walked in, the air was heavy with disappointment because waiting for me were seven of my former students who had graduated four months earlier and had yet to find nursing jobs. Their desperation was palpable. They had always been told, "Become a nurse, you will always have a job," but it was now several months after graduation and not one of them had even had an interview. I was meeting with them to rewrite their resumes, and as I turned to the internet to search a website that might help them find nursing jobs, I found none posted. I remember reflecting on my own feelings of frustration that I was unable to make a difference in the world.

I woke up from sleep later that night, turned to my husband, and said, "I know what I have to do with my life. I have to build a website to help nurses find jobs and match them with those who want to hire nurses." Not receiving the enthusiastic response I had been looking for, as he was only half-listening, I got out of bed and called my favorite nurse, who at the time and still is today, my mother. I got her on the phone and explained my idea, and she said, "That's great, but could you call me back in the morning?" I think they both hoped that in the morning, I would have slept off my great idea, but no luck—it was the beginning of my founding of HireNurses.com.

> "It's 1% inspiration, 99% perspiration."
>
> — Albert Einstein (Goodreads.com, 2019)

To me, Einstein meant that to start a company, the inspiration is only a smart part and the rest is really hard work. In a sense, innovation is the inspiration and entrepreneurship is the perspiration. Innovation becomes entrepreneurship when you decide to develop, build, fund, and scale the innovation. The idea is often the "easy" part; it is the execution of the idea that really matters. Business execution was like learning a foreign language or even two languages at the same time. As a nurse, no one had ever told me the first thing about business, finance, operations, or strategy. Part of the reason I agreed to write this chapter is so I could outline all the things I wish people had told me, which will save you the hours and hours of wasted time that I spent fumbling my way through starting a company and becoming an "entrepreneur."

What is entrepreneurship?

According to Merriam-Webster, an entrepreneur is "one who organizes, manages and assumes the risks of a business or enterprise" (para. 1 2019). Another definition is, "a person who organizes and manages any enterprise, especially a business, usually with considerable initiative and risk" (Dictionary. com, 2019). While there are many definitions of entrepreneurship, to me, it is about betting on yourself and your idea because you feel so passionately about it that you risk the safety and security of a regular job to work 100 hours a week for free. Hoping one day that it will pay off. I played it rather safe when I started my company, because my husband had a good job, and I kept working, raising three small children, and building HireNurses.com. I was working nearly 18 hours each day for a year as I spent time each evening between 9 pm and 2 am with a development company in India.

HireNurses.com almost never started. I needed funding, and as I approached my father for investment funding, he asked me whether it was such a great idea and why someone else hadn't someone else come up with it sooner. His comment stopped me in my tracks. It made me question my intelligence. Why hadn't someone smarter than me thought of this idea? If there was such a need, why didn't it already exist? Surely I must have missed something that was going to doom me to failure. That one simple question evoked such stress, fear, and doubt that I almost threw in the towel.

> *"If I had asked people what they wanted, they would have said faster horses."*
>
> *— Henry Ford, inventor of the modern day automobile (Inc.com, 2019)*

I wish I had known that quote from Henry Ford at that time. It summed up the answer in a way that I could not yet articulate. What the quote has come to mean to me is that innovation is seeing what yet does not exist, believing in a better way, and believing that you can create it. Most people will keep doing business the way it has always been done; they don't like change and can't see what has not yet been created. This is what makes entrepreneurs so amazing. Entrepreneurship is about going against the grain, challenging the status quo, getting uncomfortable, and facing the naysayers over and over again, until you find the first client who believes in your product. Some say it is luck that helps the entrepreneur in their journey, and lucky for me, my father was only half of the equation of financial support in my journey to starting a company.

My start-up funding came from my mother, who gave me her nursing retirement savings to start HireNurses™. She had worked as an oncology nurse and after both my father and my husband refused to help fund my new business, she cashed in her retirement to allow me to build the first platform. I think that is why I never gave up—I knew how hard she had worked as a nurse. In 2018, HireNurses was acquired by Ryalto, and I was able to pay my mom back her retirement savings, with a bit of interest. This was one of my proudest and greatest moments of my life. I knew that my family would never have let me live it down if I had lost her money. While HireNurses wasn't a "unicorn" (a startup worth $1B market value), it forever shaped my future and started my nursing journey down a path I would never have found without it. I am forever grateful that I took the risk, because I would not be who I am today without teetering on the brink of failure.

> **TIP**: Make sure that when you decide to start your business, you have at least one person who believes in you. You will need to rely on that person because the truth is, you will receive far many more "no's" than "yes's," and you will need support, as well as belief in yourself, to get you through the moments when things are really tough.

Entrepreneurship vs. intrapreneurship:

If you don't feel quite ready for entrepreneurship but you still want to experiment with bringing new ideas to your place of work to see how it goes, consider intrapreneurship. Intrapreneurship is when an innovation is within your place of work with a goal of driving change. If you are the type of person who is constantly coming up with new ideas at work, you are an intrapreneur! It is like entrepreneurship without the risk of leaving the security of your job. Intrapreneurship drives positive change and impacts your place of work. If you aren't ready for the risk of entrepreneurship, consider intrapreneurship and see what happens in your career. However, if you are ready to venture out onto the "road less traveled," keep going—it's time to get to work as an entrepreneur.

> *"Intrapreneurs are employees who do for corporate innovation what an entrepreneur does for his or her start-up."*
>
> *- Gifford Pinchot III (Forbes, 2019)*

Skill-building exercise: Mini-Personal-Hackathon

1. Identify a problem that you currently experience—this can be at work, at home, anywhere, really. The problem that you are identifying should cause you considerable annoyance or make you feel like you are wasting your time or that you can do "it" better.

2. Identify how you currently deal with this problem.

3. Then identify, if you had all the resources you needed, how you would deal with this problem differently.

Do this a couple of times. Make sure to think through the problem you want to solve by starting your company or patenting an idea. This will start you thinking in business terms and like an entrepreneur.

My real-life personal example:

1. *Problem*: My hospice patients couldn't find affordable care that would allow them to die at home. At the same time, new nursing graduates could not find nursing jobs.

2. *Current Solution:* Families were putting their loved ones into nursing homes. While new graduate nurses were working as restaurant servers while they looked for nursing jobs.

3. *New Solution*: This was my "aha" moment. I wondered if there was a place where nurses could connect directly with people who needed to hire nurses—a central place that worked as a matchmaking service for nurses and nursing opportunities. From that, HireNurses.com was born.

Pitfalls of the entrepreneur

Once you have an idea, have worked through a "mini-personal-hackathon," and still want to proceed as an entrepreneur, these three things will help you officially start your business.

1. *EIN (employer identification number):* This is free and comes from the federal government. This allows the business to open a bank account, pay taxes, pay employees, and set up business relationships.

2. *Register the business:* Consider different models (which will be discussed more in depth later in the book). Consider starting with an LLC. Consult an attorney to make the decision that is best for you.

3. *Business name and website:* Buy a URL (uniform resource locator). Do not pick a business name first; instead, think of a name you'd like to have. Don't get too attached to it because you may have to search through several until you find one that is available. You will also need to find a corresponding website (URL) and secure that as well. Once you secure a URL, things become real. Suddenly, the business exists and is set in motion. Your vision now has a destination.

> **Tip**: Don't hire or pay for what you can teach or learn yourself. I spent $5,000 for someone to teach me how to maximize social media and marketing for my business. It turned out to be a big waste of money. In the end, I taught myself social media via YouTube and realized that I knew my audience better than any marketer I could afford would know. Use your money wisely and learn what you don't know. The skills I taught myself when starting my business have been incredibly helpful throughout my career. See these opportunities as a way to learn new things, and you will never regret it. Hire people for the things you can't teach yourself or know you hate to do, such as filing taxes, building a website, or legal work.

One of the greatest lessons I learned as an entrepreneur is that I knew far less about many things than I ever realized. When starting a business, this is a huge challenge to overcome. Find a mentor or even several mentors to help you. When I finally launched HireNurses, I sent out an email to my nursing friends, and I did not receive any responses. I had asked them for thoughts, comments, and ideas on how to drive engagement for my new business. I considered that my dad had been right—maybe HireNurses wasn't such a great idea. Years later, as I began to build the Nurse Innovation and Entrepreneurship program at Northeastern University, I reflected on this request and realized that the lack of responses from my nursing colleagues was not because they were being mean, but because they had no idea how to start a business.

Mentors

A friend suggested that I go to SCORE, at the Small Business Association, which provides free meetings with business mentors. It was my first experience having a mentor. I must have caused my first two mentors sustained heartburn because I had no idea about what they were talking about or what they were asking me to do most of the time. The key to success is to pick one problem or a piece of a problem to resolve and then solve it well and build from there.

As an entrepreneur, it is hard not to want to create a solution that solves all the problems you see. However, success comes from small wins that build into larger ones. Now, I often find myself saying the same thing that I was told by my mentors: "Don't boil the ocean." The advice is given because to be successful, you have to start small and grow.

Mentors are people who provide insight and perspective into your business or personal development. Mentors are great to bounce ideas off of and will give you honest feedback while not discouraging your idea. A good mentor will challenge you to think differently and will help you make informed decisions. Mentors are people who have had relevant life or work experiences in the area you are hoping to succeed in. Generally, mentors become mentors because they enjoy giving back to others or paying it forward. Remember that paying it forward will go a very long way in life, so try to find mentors who feel the same way.

Board of advisors

A board of advisors is slightly different than mentors, as they are individuals whom you appoint to your board for a small amount of equity (value) in your business. A board of advisors is strategically appointed due to the "gravitas" and "connections" that their association with your company will bring. Mentors can often morph into your board of advisors later as your business progresses.

Finding the right mentors early on in your entrepreneurship journey will set you on the right path for success. Mentors will serve as your greatest sounding board and will be the best investment of your time as you are building your business. My first two mentors led me to find more mentors. I can't tell you how life changing they were to my journey as an entrepreneur, and they are still my dearest friends.

TIP: Find mentors whom you like, want to emulate, and even aspire to be one day. Don't keep company with people who make you feel bad about yourself. Mentors are confident in who they are and what they have accomplished. Know that you will fail, pivot, and fail again on the road to success.

"I work really hard at trying to see the big picture and not getting stuck in ego. I believe we are all put on this planet for a purpose, and we all have a different purpose . . . when you connect with that love and compassion, that's when everything else unfolds."

— Ellen DeGeneres, comedian (articles.bplans.com, 2019)

I was not prepared for the amount of failure I would experience on my entrepreneurship journey. The number of "no's," the phone hang-ups, and the feeling like I was a *persona non-grata* at so many meetings were all hard to deal with. The old saying, "one step forward and two steps back," is a constant in the world of entrepreneurship. The highs are so high and the lows so low, it's an endless rollercoaster of emotions. Be sure to follow a few of the tips in Chapter 2 to help you through this part of the entrepreneurship journey.

The most successful entrepreneurs have faced great challenges and failures as they built their business. However, failure for them was not the end, but the start of a transformation. If the path toward success was a consistent formula, everyone would do it. What makes a successful entrepreneur unique is that there is no such a formula. Success is about "grit," the ability to deal with getting knocked down and getting back up. It's a test of inner strength, fortitude, and belief in yourself and what you are building. If you ever played sports or were on a team, you have probably experienced a time when you lost a game. Those bitter lessons that were gained from the loss made you better and stronger in the end. The lessons you learn from not quitting after loss can help you prepare for a journey into entrepreneurship. The most important lessons in life are learned from failures and losses because they teach that disappointment can be overcome.

"With great risk, comes great reward."

— Thomas Jefferson (Establishconnections.com, 2013)

A common thread among entrepreneurs is that they often view the world as "a glass is half full." How you view the world is very important on your journey of entrepreneurship. Discouragement and bad days are prevalent, and you may want to throw in the towel—yet the next day, you wake up and are back at it. As nurses, we do this every day of our career. We have the unique opportunity to care for people who are experiencing the worst times of their lives, and we face it head on, helping them through these moments. As a nurse, you already have the inner strength you need to survive life as entrepreneur. There couldn't be a better career to get you prepared for the life of an entrepreneur than nursing.

Unfortunately, it is not very well known that there is a long legacy of amazing nurse entrepreneurs and innovators, who are finally being recognized for their innovations from decades ago. Nursing is changing, and the possibilities of what we can do with our career is entering a phase unlike any before in the nursing profession. A new era of nurse scientists, innovators, designers, informaticists, inventors, entrepreneurs, and leaders are redefining the future of what is possible for nurses and reshaping the healthcare landscape. There has never been more opportunity for the future of the nursing profession than there is today. *Carpe diem*, fellow nurses: we only live once, so let's make it count. Go forth to change the world, for there is no one more qualified or with truer intentions to make the world a better place than nurses.

If you are ready to start on your own entrepreneurial journey, check out SONSIEL.com: (Society of Nurse Scientists, Innovators, Entrepreneurs & Leaders). These are nurses who have created a non-profit organization to support nurses across the world in their own innovation and entrepreneurial journeys! We look forward to welcoming you to our "tribe"!

References

Articles.bplans.com. (2019). Ellen DeGeneres quote. Accessed on March 19, 2019. Accessed at https://articles.bplans.com/21-quotes-women-thrive-as-entrepreneurs/.

Bigcommerce.com. (2019). Accessed on March 19, 2019. Accessed at https://www.bigcommerce.com/blog/quotes-for-entrepreneurs/.

Establishconnections.com. (2013). Thomas Jefferson quote. Accessed on March 19, 2019. Accessed at https://establishconnections.wordpress.com/2013/09/23/with-great-risk-comes-great-reward-t-jefferson/.

Forbes. (January 8, 2019). Intrapreneurship. Accessed on March 25, 2019. Accessed at https://www.forbes.com/sites/jordandaykin/2019/01/08/intrapreneurship/#22c6b2984ea3.

Goodreads.com. (2019). Albert Einstein quote. Accessed on March 19, 2019. Accessed at https://www.goodreads.com/quotes/115696-genius-is-1-talent-and-99-percent-hard-work.

Inc.com. (2019). Henry Ford quote. Accessed on March 19, 2019. Accessed at https://www.inc.com/michael-graber/people-would-have-asked-for-faster-horses-henry-fords-dilemma.html.

Merriam-Webster.com. (2019). Definition of entrepreneur. Accessed on March 19, 2019. Accessed at https://www.merriam-webster.com/dictionary/entrepreneurship?utm_campaign=sd&utm_medium=serp&utm_source=jsonld.

Dictionary.com. (2019).Definition of entrepreneur. Accessed on March 19, 2019. Accessed at https://www.dictionary.com/browse/entrepreneur.

4 Building a Business Case

By Dr. Bonnie Clipper

Objectives

By the end of this chapter, the reader will be able to:

• Explain the importance of using empathy to define a problem.

• Develop a Lean Canvas for a specific business idea.

• Describe the design thinking process and how it can be used to solve a problem or frame up a business opportunity.

> "Your work is going to fill a large part of your life, and the only way to be truly satisfied is to do what you believe is great work. And the only way to do great work is to love what you do." — Steve Jobs (oberlo.com, 2018)

Due to the sheer number of nurses, as well as their increasing presence in other industries, opportunities have never been better for nurses to develop solutions and start a business. Nurses are continually shifting their influence into different areas. While the traditional roles for nurses are within healthcare organizations, such as hospitals and clinics, nurses are now working as informaticists, data scientists, remotely as virtual care nurses, and even as designers who are influencing technology. This all means that nurses are well positioned to meet market demands and start new businesses.

Consider the training that nurses undergo just to be able to take the licensure exam and how the holistic approach to dealing not only with patients but also their support systems and general environments can be an asset as a business person. Nurses are well prepared to become business owners and entrepreneurs.

Additionally, the demographic shift is presenting a "perfect storm" of opportunity for nurses due to this unique skill set. Consider that by 2030, for the first time in our history, there will be more residents who are sixty-five years old and older than there will be children (AARP 2018).

In addition to the change in demographics, life expectancy has increased as well. In 1972, someone who was sixty-five could expect to live an average of fifteen more years, which increased to an additional nineteen years by 2010 (Census.gov, 2014). Even more impressive is the increase in life expectancy from someone who is age eighty-five. In 1972, the average eight-five-year-old could expect to live five more years, while in 2010, the average eighty-five-year-old could expect an additional 6.5 years (Census.gov, 2014).

As we continue to see an increase in the number of people aging, we know that this demographic will transform not only the way care is delivered but also our expectations of aging and health overall. Think about the needs of this dramatically changing group and the business opportunities as a result of an increased demand for people to age in place. This is just one strong example where nurses can make an incredible impact through innovation and are perfectly positioned for entrepreneurship, or entreprenurses.

Developing a business model

When looking at the opportunities that exist for nurses, it is important to understand how to start a business. The smartest way to start a business is with a business plan. Starting a business is serious stuff and is not the time to "wing it." It is important to develop a business plan that will provide the opportunity to be thoughtful about the journey and shape what the business looks like before the work begins. One of the best ways to approach a business plan is to use a process called Lean Canvas. Lean Canvas is based on the Business Model Canvas and was adapted by Ash Maurya (Leanstack.com, 2018). Lean Canvas is a brilliant approach to developing business plans. In the past, writing a business plan could have taken days or possibly even weeks. Lean Canvas provides an opportunity to write a business plan in less than an hour. While business plans are continually refined based on the changing environment and business dynamics, this is a great approach to get started. The nine steps of Lean Canvas will be explained with an opportunity to practice the newly learned skills.

Leanstack.com is a great source to use to build a Lean Canvas. This site provides blank templates and resources to develop customized plans. Using a template such as this and committing about an hour of time will help get ideas on paper. If it takes longer, that is fine too. Start with sticky notes or a whiteboard or directly on the Leanstack.com site, the important thing is just to start. This is a great way to capture the thoughts necessary to develop something for friends, family, and even colleagues to react to. It sounds much harder than it is. Going through this process will save time later because it will force all these hard questions up front and get them down in one place for further discussion. While it's tempting to start with a solution, it is very important to first start with the right problem.

Skill-building exercise:

Use the template below to develop your own Lean Canvas for your business idea.

1 Problem

Start with the problem that you want to solve. This is truly the most critical stage. This isn't about you wanting to start a business, but rather the problem that needs to be solved. Be sure to think about this carefully. So often, we find "solutions" that really don't have a problem associated with them.

2 Customer segments

Think of the appropriate customers who have this problem and will benefit from a solution. Are your customers nurses? Hospitals? Patients? Think carefully about whom the solution is targeted to.

3 Unique value proposition

This is the value that you intend to deliver. This is the reason a customer should buy from you. Think about what makes you different in this space. Be critical: Why would someone give their money to you?

PROBLEM	SOLUTION	UNIQUE VALUE PROPOSITION	UNFAIR ADVANTAGE	CUSTOMER SEGMENTS
	KEY METRICS		CHANNELS	
EXISTING ALTERNATIVES		HIGH-LEVEL CONCEPT		EARLY ADOPTERS

COST STRUCTURE	REVENUE STREAMS

(Maurya, A. 2019. Lean Canvas is adapted from The Business Model Canvas and is licensed under the Creative Commons Attribution-Share Alike 3.0 Un-ported License)

4   Solution

What is the solution that you bring to this problem? This may change over time because solutions are dynamic. And that's okay. As you learn more about your customers and your solution, this may be a moving target.

5   Channels

How is your solution going to reach your customers? How will you distribute to and reach your customers? What will give you enough access to your customers? Is it email? Social media? Exhibiting at conferences? Webinars? Consider where your customers are and how you can reach them.

6   Revenue streams

How are you going to determine pricing for your goods or services? It's not uncommon for new businesses or startups to provide things at a very low cost or even free in the beginning. The strategy here is to gain traction while you are building a customer base. Will there be one revenue stream or more than one?

7   Cost structure

Think about the costs you are going to incur for building this business, whether it's a product or service. What are all the costs associated with your new business? Will you have a brick-and-mortar office or store? Or will this be virtual? How much are you going to spend on marketing? What are your production costs? What about labor costs? Supply costs? Insurance costs? All these things have to be considered when you determine your cost structure.

8   Key metrics

What are the metrics that will be used to determine your company's success? Is it revenue? Social media impressions? Month-over-month sales numbers? Blog posts? These are important things that need to be considered to determine whether your company is headed in the right direction.

9   Unfair advantage

Carefully consider why someone should buy from you and only you. What gives you an unfair advantage in this segment or industry? This is different than your Unique Value Proposition. This is something that is an advantage to you because it cannot be copied or bought anywhere else. Do you have something that no one else can sell? This is the hardest question to answer on the Lean Canvas template. This is your opportunity to think about what makes you so awesome. And this is your chance to use your superpower as a nurse.

"People ignore design that ignores people."

— *Frank Chimero (Howdesign.com, 2018)*

Design thinking

Another tool to help you as you consider building a business, whether it's for a product or service, is to incorporate design thinking. Design thinking, also known as human-centered design (HCD), was developed into a tool for collaborative problem solving by IDEO in the 1990s (designthinking.ideo.com, 2019). It is fascinating to think that architecture, furniture and interior design, and even aviation have adopted the HCD approach well ahead of the healthcare industry. Ironically, health care is the most human-centered of all industries yet has been the last to consider HCD as an approach to problem-solving and designing care processes.

Design thinking model

In the design thinking model, there are three components of equal value that when they intersect, (like a Venn diagram) provide the "sweet spot" for innovation to occur. These three components are:

*   **desirability**: the human component that is important to understand in terms of what people want and what makes sense

*   **feasibility**: the technicality of what is possible

*   **viability**: a business component that inquires as to what is likely to become part of the business model

Essential aspects of design thinking

Using design thinking in a new business startup endeavor makes a great deal of sense. Design thinking starts by questioning whether the correct problem is being solved by ensuring that the customers are truly understood. According to Ideo, a well-known expert in the design thinking world, there are three essential aspects in design thinking. These include empathy, ideation, and experimentation (Ideo, 2018). As nurses, we are well prepared from an empathy and compassion perspective. We are generally very adept at looking at a person as a "whole" and trying to understand them, as well as their environment. In fact, nearly all nurses are taught Watson's Caring Theory, which focuses on enhancing human dignity, respect for "the person," and connecting with human beings as a person (Watsoncaringscience.org, 2019). As natural innovators, ideation (or brainstorming) is a skill that is common as critical thinking, another skill that is hard wired in nurses. In the nursing world, "experimentation" is a reference to trying to see what works, as we often have to find novel ways to do things or accomplish our work.

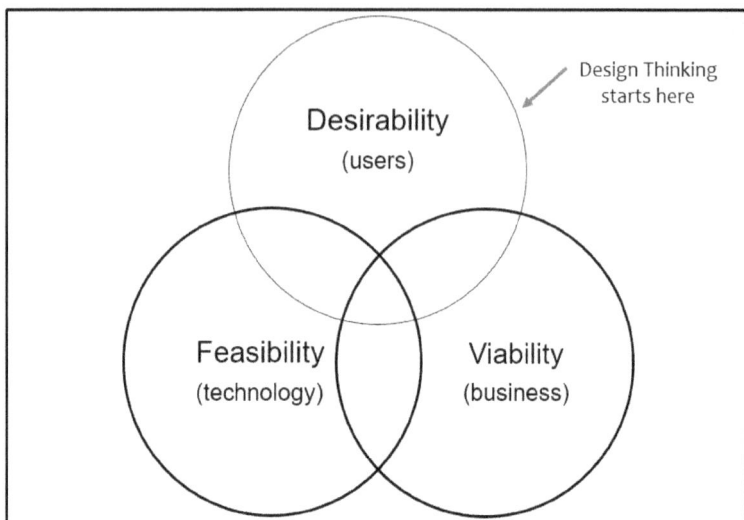

(Zuber, 2019)

Five steps of the design thinking process

There are five steps often associated with the design thinking process. These are more detailed than the Essential Aspects of Design Thinking. The five steps include: empathy, define, ideate, prototype, and test.

Empathy

This means digging deep into what you think the problem is and asking yourself, "Why is this a problem?" at least five more times. It is important to *empathize* to truly understand the problem you are trying to solve. As nurses, not only do we have an incredible sense of critical thinking and problem solving, we are also very empathetic. This makes us rock stars when using the design thinking process.

Define

Clarity around defining the problem is essential. We learned earlier about the importance of understanding the problem in using the Lean Canvas to build a business model. There is no step more important than clearly defining and understanding the problem.

Ideate

This is the fun step. Ideating, also known as brainstorming, allows the opportunity for divergent thinking. This is the opportunity to consider any aspects of the problem or solution, no matter how wacky or extraneous. Write any ideas on sticky notes and place them on the wall. Stare at the ideas for a long time. Don't start filtering ideas out at this stage (Cianelli, Clipper, Freeman, Goldstein & Wyatt, 2015). As you zero in on solutions, they will become clear as you move on to the next step.

Prototype

Prototyping provides the opportunity to use arts and crafts supplies, 3D printers, duct tape, and anything else that can be used to develop a prototype. This is the first chance to really "build" what the product might look like. This is also known as a Minimum Viable Product (MVP). It doesn't have to be "pretty" or good looking at this stage, just functional. This is the opportunity to prototype something and is generally a fairly rapid process.

Test (similar to experimentation)

In this stage, testing is the ability to try out the prototyped solution to see how it works. Failure is good! The saying goes, "Fail fast and fail often." That means get failure out of the way in the early stages so you can continue to iterate and work toward a solution that actually makes sense, functions properly, and looks like it will truly solve the problem you started out intending to solve. When we fail, we need to learn from our failures and quickly adjust and move on. In fact, there are many organizations that view failure as exciting and as much an opportunity as success. One great example of this is at tech companies, where the recognition of failure often helps ensure that there is still room to celebrate innovation and disruption in the future. Failure means that people are willing to try something new and to think out of the box. If we are all too afraid to fail, it means we aren't really being disruptive and thinking in a new way.

Just to be clear, testing or experimentation is *never* intended to jeopardize patient care or safety. It is intended for the small "tests" that we might perform to try out new processes that will help us transform care, such as testing an app. or testing a new workflow. Any testing that might involve patients needs to be very carefully planned and go through the appropriate process, such as an Institutional Review Board (IRB) review and approval process.

The design thinking process is a great way to think about solving problems in healthcare or in anything, for that matter. There are also parallels between design thinking and the nursing process. A well-known nurse practitioner colleague once said:

Assessing requires Empathizing
Diagnosing can be thought of as Defining
Planning is like Ideating
Implementing requires Prototyping
Evaluating is similar to Testing.
(Hendler, N., Personal communication, November 13, 2018)

Skill-building exercise:

Use the five steps of the design thinking process to define a problem that you have identified, and ideate through ten potential solutions, coming up with a potential action to test. This is your chance to use sticky notes and colored markers and come up with how you might solve this challenge. Is there a business opportunity in this for you?

"Design is not a single object or dimension. Design is messy and complex."

— Natasha Jen *(Howdesign.com, 2018)*

Call to action:

Utilize the output from the skill-building opportunity above, and build a business model using Lean Canvas. Be clear and thoughtful about the problem you are solving. Share your plan with your most trusted friends and family to solicit feedback. Is there really an opportunity for you? Can you build a revenue-generating business as a result?

There has never been a better time for nurses to use their skills and expertise to develop successful businesses. Learning the tools described in this chapter, such as Lean Canvas and applying the design thinking process, will provide solid footing to start on the journey of being a business owner or entreprenurse. Don't hold back. The hardest part is to get started.

References

AARP (2018). Age 65+ Adults Are Projected to Outnumber Children by 2030. Accessed on February 23, 2019. Accessed at https://www.aarp.org/home-family/friends-family/info-2018/census-baby-boomers-fd.htm.
An Aging Nation: The Older Population in the United States (2014). Accessed on February 23, 2019. Accessed at https://www.census.gov/prod/2014pubs/p25-1140.pdf.

Cianelli, R., Clipper, B., Freeman, R., Goldstein, J. & Wyatt, T. (2016). *The Innovation Road Map: A Guide for Nurse Leaders*. Greensboro, NC. Published by Innovation Works.

Designthinking.ideo.com (2019). Design Thinking Model. Accessed on February 23, 2019. Accessed at https://designthinking.ideo.com/.

Ideo. (2018). Accessed on February 23, 2019. Accessed at (https://www.ideou.com/blogs/inspiration/what-is-design-thinking.

Hendler, N. (November 13, 2018). Personal communication.

Howdesign.com. (2018) Frank Chimero quote. Accessed on February 23, 2019. Accessed at https://www.howdesign.com/conference-news/how-design-live/quotes-about-design-how-design-live-2017/.

Howdesign.com. (2018) Natasha Jen quote. Accessed on February 23, 2019. Accessed at https://www.howdesign.com/conference-news/how-design-live/quotes-about-design-how-design-live-2017/.

Leanstack.com (2018). Accessed on February 23, 2019. Accessed at https://www.leanstack.com.

Oberlo.com (2018). Steve Jobs quote. Accessed on February 23, 2019. Accessed at https://www.oberlo.com/blog/best-inspirational-business-quotes.

Watsoncaringscience.org (2019). Watson's Theory of Caring. Accessed on February 24, 2019 at https://www.watsoncaringscience.org/.

Zuber, C., Personal communication, May 29, 2019

5 Intellectual Property, Patents, and Trademarks

By Michael Wang and Dr. Paul Coyne

Objectives

By the end of this chapter, the reader will be able to:

- Articulate an understanding of the important aspects of an intellectual property strategy.

- Describe a step-by-step process of what it takes to establish sound protection.

- Explain the various terms associated with intellectual property protection, such as non-disclosure agreements, trademarks, and provisional and non-provisional patents.

  "He who receives an idea from me, receives instruction himself without lessening mine; as he who lights his taper at mine, receives light without darkening me."

  — Thomas Jefferson (Goodreads.com, 2018)

At this point in your innovation journey, you have developed an idea that you have determined is worth pursuing. If an innovation/invention is deemed worthy of your time, energy, and money, it is important enough for you to protect. Your idea, also known as intellectual property (IP), may have real monetary value, as we discussed in Chapter One. Intellectual property is "any product of the human intellect that the law protects from unauthorized use by others and is traditionally comprised of four categories: patent, copyright, trademark, and trade secrets" (law.cornell.edu, 2018, para.1). Just as you wouldn't leave the door to your house unlocked, you should take all appropriate steps to protect your idea.

Patents

Before you start thinking about protecting your idea, you must be careful to ensure that the idea is truly yours. Consider this: if you find a puppy on the side of the road, what do you do? Do you take him home and invest the time and energy into loving it, only to have someone claim him a week later? The first thing you *should* do is check the collar and see if this puppy already belongs to someone else. The same thought should occur when you come up with a good idea. If you begin devoting your resources and energy to an idea that is not yours, you will be very frustrated when someone claims the idea later. You must make sure your idea is not infringing upon someone else's in any way. The only way to know if an idea has already been developed is to read the relevant patents. A patent is legal evidence that the individual granted the patent has "exclusive right to exclude others from making, using, importing, and selling the patented innovation for a limited period of time" (law.cornell.edu, 2018, para.2).

> **Skill-building exercise:** Go online to the United States Patent Office Database (USPTO.gov), and search for some of your favorite products in the patent database. Identify those that are interesting, and read a few of the patents for these products. Take time to review the content and how they are written.

Patents serve a specific purpose in that they detail the design and application of the invention. As important as it is to protect your ideas, it is equally important to ensure that your idea does not infringe upon those of others, as this could sidetrack your own idea. Contrary to popular belief, there are various levels of intellectual property protection that you can seek. This is true even if you have limited financial resources.

Consider your goal when purchasing a car; it may start with the basic desire to have the means to get from point A to point B. Depending on how much money you spend on this purchase and what risks you are willing to accept, your choices will be either vast or limited. No matter what choice you make, you will still get from point A to point B, whether you drive a Rolls Royce or a Honda. If an accident happens along the way, your risks are adjusted accordingly, depending on what kind of car you invested in. The same is true of intellectual property protection. A patent is one way to do this.

In order to file a patent, you do not need to have a marketable product completed. The purpose of patent filing is:

- exclusive rights
- strong market position
- higher returns on investments
- opportunity to license or sell the invention

- increase in negotiating

- positive image for your enterprise

(WIPO.int, 2019)

If your financial resources are limited, it is not necessary to invest in a robust patent strategy. Instead, invest in IP protection that you feel meets the need and that you can afford. The cost for IP protection can range from two hundred dollars to millions of dollars. You should consult an attorney who has IP experience to help advise you on the best course of action. Be sure to talk to a few different attorneys to learn about their experience and the quality of their work.

During the golden age of technological development (which includes the steam engine, automobile, and factory equipment), designing and obtaining utility patents immediately was of crucial importance for someone like Edison or Tesla in their quest to dominate market share. However, as we entered the digital age, a phased strategy encompassing software protection, both in the form of utility and design patents, as well as trade secrets, became more feasible as the market became more complex.

> **Call to action**: Define your idea (the one you started earlier in the book), and ensure that you are able to articulate your idea backward and forward so anyone can understand it. Practice it over and over, in the mirror if necessary. It has to roll off your tongue.

Protecting your intellectual property starts as soon as you have derived (developed) an idea, articulated it, drawn it out, and discovered that it is unique. Be careful not to give away your excitement at this stage; you must contain yourself. Do not call your colleagues and friends and show them your napkin sketch. You must limit the scope of your discussions with others or ensure that you have protections in place with other investors, customers, or others who may have an interest in your idea.

Non-disclosure agreement

A non-disclosure agreement (NDA) and the execution of these documents is a common practice that memorializes conversations between people who agree, whether unilaterally or mutual, to not share a particular idea and any discussions they have with each other pertaining to that idea. There are a variety of NDAs; we are going to talk about the most "simple" one.

> **Call to action**: Whenever you have an idea that you think may be novel and unique, send an email to yourself. This is a time-stamped way of proving you thought of it on a certain date and time. Send yourself an email right now of the idea you are going to try to build a business out of or commercialize.

As you complete an application for the NDA, it is important that you write as much detail as possible. Focus broadly—do not only include the current application and purpose of your solution but also any potential future application that may be enabled by future developments in other technology that will unlock the full potential of your current idea. Think big. This does not need to be in physical form nor does it need to be an actual product that is market ready. Just protect anything that you can imagine as a result of this idea/innovation.

Case study:

When Inspiren was in its early days, we paid $500 for basic online protection service to ensure that we had a time-stamped date of our most basic ideas. Our very first application was a provisional patent. In this provisional patent, which we wrote much of ourselves, we outlined our ideas that were not technical in nature but were effective in communicating the functionality. Keep in mind that at this point, we had no prototype and no product. As a matter of fact, we did not even have a team to assemble this product. We just wrote a provisional patent of our ideas. In doing so, our valuation increased, our idea was protected, and we were able to articulate our vision to investors, our development team, and most importantly, ourselves. In many ways, our lack of technical expertise regarding computer hardware and software freed our minds from the technological limitations at the time. Our ignorance allowed us to think beyond what others may have thought possible.

This case study demonstrates a critical part of the process. By putting your ideas down in a patent application, you are forced to visualize the product roadmap several years down the road. Do not be limited by current reality in the patent. Write as if everything your solution could become if not limited by technology will happen. In doing so, you will simultaneously plan a future roadmap and protect yourself.

Provisional patent

This is analogous to writing a business plan before a business is created. Another critical purpose to a patent application, even a provisional patent, is that this allows you to have leverage during the investment and fundraising process. A provisional patent is "a patent application that can be used by a patent applicant to secure a filing date while avoiding the costs associated with the filing and prosecution of a non-provisional patent application" (uspto.gov, 2018, para. 2).

You may file the patent prior to the formation of a business entity. However, it is in your best interest to file this as individuals and then later "assign" it to the company. This helps later and can be used as a bargaining chip during the fundraising negotiations. Any sophisticated investor will require the founders to transfer all IP over to the company so the IP is not held by individuals. In certain instances, it may also be beneficial to create an independent LLC whose sole purpose is to hold the IP of your invention. The benefits of doing so are to protect the IP as an isolated, independent business entity. Knowing all this, you are now ready to take the first step and file your provisional patent.

There are key differences between provisional and non-provisional patents. A provisional patent is shorter in nature and far less expensive. It is also a great way to begin your thinking process while buying you more time to protect your idea and proving (from a legal perspective) that your idea was established and registered with the United States Patent Office. The US Patent Office is the federal agency for granting US patents and registering trademarks. In doing this, the USPTO fulfills the mandate of Article I, Section 8, Clause 8, of the Constitution that the legislative branch "promote the Progress of Science and useful Arts, by securing for limited Times to Authors and Inventors the exclusive Right to their respective Writings and Discoveries" (uspto.gov, 2018, para.1).

This protects you in the event that there is a discrepancy regarding claims of "who came up with the idea first." Another major difference in the two types of patents is time. A provisional patent provides a year of discretion as you decide whether to proceed to a non-provisional patent or to discontinue pursuing a patent. Another advantage to a provisional patent is that it is not "searchable," or open to the public, within the year it is filed. This protects the idea from "visibility" to those who may be searching for new patents or ideas.

Trade secret

In the realm of protection of ideas, at times, a non-provisional patent could be a double-edged sword. It is important to consider whether your idea or invention should be patented or kept as a trade secret. A trade secret "derives independent economic value, actual or potential, from not being generally known to, and not being readily ascertainable by proper means by, other persons who can obtain economic value from its disclosure or use; and is the subject of efforts that are reasonable under the circumstances to maintain its secrecy" (law.cornell.edu, 2018, para.2).

A great example is Coca-Cola. The formula for this drink has never been patented. It has been kept as a trade secret because once a non-provisional is filed, the contents of patent becomes public information. Before doing anything, it is important to ask yourself: "Do I want others to gain detailed access to my idea and my invention?" Ask your IP attorney to help you in this process.

To answer this question, you must consider whether the release of this information will help your competitors make a better, competing product. A patent is never a guarantee. It simply a form of protection. Just like there is really no such thing as a "bulletproof vest"—with the right caliber of bullet, anything is penetrable. And with the right kind of legal workaround, a similar technology can circumvent your patent for a competitor. When filing the provisional patent, it is required that all people who contributed to the invention be listed as part of the patent application. To avoid any future disagreements between inventors, it is advisable for all inventors to agree to assign IP to the business entity. The last thing you want is not being able to get funded or sell your business because one individual/inventor disagrees with a business decision of the rest of the group and refuses to assign.

If you are further along in the development process or you have already developed a working prototype or marketable product, it is important to differentiate between those who are hired to work on your product and those who actually invented it. It is important to emphasize that any vendor that works on your invention includes a "work for hire" clause within their development contract. This clause essentially means that any work completed or that is derived from the completing of your product belongs to you and your company, not the vendor.

In all development contracts with vendors or any that include "work for hire," it is critical that this clause is in a signed agreement. Do not sign any contracts without this clause. This is extremely important because as a product is being developed, additional new ideas and improvements to your initial idea will occur. In anticipation of such changes and modifications, you must create a predevelopment understanding of the IP assignment in writing, prior to the commencement of work. If it isn't in writing, signed by all parties, then no protections exist.

> *"At his best, man is the noblest of all animals: separated from law and justice, he is the worst."*

> — Aristotle *(Brainyquotes.com, 2018)*

IP protection in the form of a trade secret, or a non-provisional patent, is not the only form of protection that is needed for your brand and company. It is easy to have the mindset that the chances of your brand becoming a household name is rare. However, in the eventuality of your success, it becomes critically important to protect your brand's name, description, logo design, and identity. Think about how many times throughout the day you use the words, "Kleenex®," "Post-it®," "Google," and "Uber." The ultimate sign of your success is when your product becomes a "verb" or defines an action in the lives of everyday people.

Protecting the brand

In addition to the design and utility protection of your actual invention, it is well worth the effort to also protect the brand, which is essentially the face of your product and ultimately, product line. This takes place in the form of copyright and trademarks. The diligence required to trademark your brand and to copyright proprietary information is critical, not only in the sense of intellectual property, but it can also directly impact your revenue and market share in terms of your ability to license proprietary information or original thinking.

An inexpensive way to protect your brand at the onset of your journey is to obtain web domains, email, Facebook, Instagram, Twitter, and other social media channels with your product and company name as soon as they are known. These names are part of your brand as well. In fact, many people make a living buying web domains they think may be worth something later and reselling them.

Even something as seemingly trivial as a simple presentation that describes your product or articulates the specific process or training involved with your product could potentially fall under copyright protection and give you the right to claim any benefit that others may gain from using such material. Whether it is a logo on a T-shirt, coffee mug, or race car, your brand communicates the value and status associated with your company. In many instances, it is just as, if not more, important than the product itself. If you have a well-known brand and an easily recognizable logo, it is often perceived more valuable than an identical product without this branding.

Hopefully, by this time, the diligence that you have devoted to thinking through the provisional patents, trademarks, and copyrights will help you receive preliminary funding, which will allow you to proceed to the next step of filing a non-provisional patent. Like many things in life, you are only as good as those whom you surround yourself with. Just as you would not buy from the first person who tries to sell you a vehicle, you also need to diligently select the right IP team to draft and file your patent.

IP legal team

It is not good enough to find an IP legal team who knows how to file a patent. It is critically important to find legal representation that has both filing and litigation experience. Just knowing how file an application does not give an attorney the skills to be able to defend one. Make sure your legal team understands the process of both prosecution and defense. It is highly recommended that you interview multiple IP firms prior to hiring one for your innovation/invention. Most IP firms offer free consultations, where you will have the chance to speak in detail concerning your invention, scope of work, cost structure, and projected fees. It is vital that you pick an IP team that has expertise in your area of invention. Nurse translation: you would not want to see a GI specialist for your chest pain. The areas of law specialties are as diverse as any other profession. Please do you and your company a favor by not asking a real estate attorney to file your patent application.

Once you have picked your legal team, make sure you thoroughly understand the way you are being charged. Standard practice involves an agreed retainer, of which you are charged against at an hourly basis. Make sure your contractual agreement stipulates your right to receive updates on the rate of your cash burn (spend) from the legal team, as well as itemized, line-by-line breakdowns of where their time was spent. It is also wise to ensure that you receive a general range of how much the total costs will be for the scope of services needed to file the patent at the onset, and you should be proactive to measure current spend against final projections throughout the process.

During patent composition, there will be many strategies and crossroads that you will need to make, which will impact the outcome of the patent. One of the first things your legal team will do is perform a "prior art search." This is where the team identifies current patents that are in existence, that may be roadblocks, or that represent potential infringement.

IP strategy

Your IP strategy must not be formulated in isolation. Every step of the patent creation must be guided by the actual results of the art search, which will dictate the manner that you will describe your invention. It is important to remember that no art search, regardless of how extensive the resources devoted to it, will ever be risk proof. It is always possible that between the time of your filing and actually receiving the patent, other products or competing brands may be file additional patents unbeknownst to you. The benefits of the provisional patent remain invisible to the public for up to one year. This also applies to your potential competitors. Therefore, it is of critical importance that you develop your IP strategy considering the multifaceted nature of patent types, as well as a variety of approaches. The same plans you will use to defend yourself will also be used by others to defend against you. However, regardless of how little or extensive your art search is, it is always better to not go in blind. In this scenario, ignorance is far from bliss.

During the IP strategy drafting process, there will be many iterations, adjustments, and adaptations to your original draft. Realize that no one will care for your product as much as you will. You must relentlessly push, criticize, and practice diligence when reviewing the draft of your patent. No detail is too small. No idea is too abstract.

When drafting your patent, there are two different strategies of attack, which you must carefully decide between.

Strategy A: This is a good approach if you have limited financial resources. In this strategy, one encompassing patent will create a general umbrella of protection for an overall concept or idea that may contain sublevel claims. The reason that this approach is preferable for those with financial restraints is due to one patent having minimal filing fees. The benefit of this approach is that you are afforded general protection while minimizing expenditure and still retaining the option to file future patents on your sublevel claims. This "wide net" approach could be effective and economical.

Strategy B: If you are less restrained by financial resources, you may choose to individually file multiple claims involved with your invention. Each claim requires its own application, filing fee, and legal fees associated with the drafting and submission. The benefit of this strategy is to be able to provide detailed protection in all various aspects of your invention, in that they can be separated, isolated, and protected independently from one another, providing additional protection if one claim is disputed. It is important to realize that the true cost of patent application does not only involve the first filing. Upon review, it is a standard practice that the US Patent Office will require that you defend certain aspects of the claims. It is this back-and-forth process that could become very costly. Therefore, ensure that your cost projection incorporates subsequent legal work and not just the initial filing. It is due to this subsequent legal work that makes implementing the numerous claim strategy exponentially more costly.

Now that you have filed your provisional and non-provisional patent, you should be good to go, right? Not so fast. Realize that patent creation with competition can be a war of attrition. As disheartening as it may be, big and powerful companies can often derail the process of a smaller company or prevent that smaller company from being a major competitor by "tying them down" in patent court. Typically, the litigating party has no interest in actually winning. As they have more financial capital, their sole intention and purpose is to exhaust your financial resources, where you have no choice but to reach a settlement. Cynical as it may be, this is a popular strategy used by large companies every day.

Armed with this knowledge, it is wise to revisit your decision of patents vs trade secrets frequently. This is an important and personal decision that you, the inventor and leader of your company, must weigh heavily, as it has great repercussions on the success of your future business.

It is also important to research and study the overall IP landscape and market of your industry. For example, if your idea is to create another coffee maker, you must realize the extensive number of existing products that will limit the potential for you to receive a successful claim. However, if your idea is so unique that a saturated market does not yet exist, it is imperative that you lay claim to this "new found market" by establishing a well-protected application.

Here is an entrepreneur's checklist for IP protection. Keep in mind that this is not all encompassing, but it does establish a foundation that will guide your thinking and your actions.

- Do you have a thorough understanding of your concept?
- Can you clearly articulate your concept?
- Have you become comfortable reading patents and understanding them?
- Have you identified a service or resource that can help you prepare your non-provisional patent?
- Have you considered at least three of these services by comparing prices, capabilities, and fit?
- Have you conducted a preliminary art search by querying the US Patent Office database independently?
- Did you determine if your invention is more suited for a trade secret or a patent, which is public?
- Are all inventors aligned and in agreement to assign IP to the company?
- Does a clear IP provision within your contacts with development partners exist?

- Have you categorized items that belong to trademark, copyright, and patent protection?

- Did you identify the appropriate legal resource and representation to file your non-provisional patent?

- Have you meticulously critiqued your patent drafts and communicated in detail these findings with your legal team?

- Have you diligently examined the competitive landscape and the potential roadblocks that you may encounter during the application process and beyond?

Conclusion

While the complexity surrounding the various legal implications outlined in this chapter may feel daunting, do not let it prevent you from starting the journey. Take one step at a time. No matter how educated and informed others are on specific portions of your innovation journey, no one will be as invested in or have as in-depth of an understanding of your innovation and business as you. This applies to attorneys as well. Devote yourself to understanding, as best you can, the intricacies of what you are signing and what your protection and risks are when signing each document. Ask as many questions as you wish, and never agree to anything unless you are comfortable. If you take the same spirit you have when you advocate for your patient and apply it to advocating for your innovation and business, you will do great!

Reference List

BrainyQuotes.com (2019) Aristotle. Accessed on March 25, 2019. Retrieved from https://www.brainyquote.com/quotes/aristotle_148472?src=t_law.

GoodReads.com (2018). Thomas Jefferson. Accessed on on March 25, 2019. Retrieved from https://www.goodreads.com/quotes/4276-he-who-receives-an-idea-from-me-receives-instruction-himself.

Law.Cornell.com (2018) Accessed on March 25, 2019. Retrieved from https://www.law.cornell.edu/wex/intellectual_property.

Law.Cornell.com (2018) Accessed on March 25, 2019. Retrieved from https://www.law.cornell.edu/wex/patent.

Law.Cornell.com (2018) Accessed on March 25, 2019. Retrieved from https://www.law.cornell.edu/wex/trade_secret.

Uspto.gov (2018) Accessed on March 25, 2019. Retrieved from https://www.uspto.gov/learning-and-resources/newsletter/inventors-eye/provisional-patent-application-what-you-need-know.

Uspto.gov (2018) Accessed on March 25, 2019. Retrieved from https://www.uspto.gov/about-us.

WIPO.int. (2019). Accessed on March 26, 2019. Retrieved from https://www.wipo.int/sme/en/ip_business/importance/reasons.htm.

6

Funding and Commercializing

By Dr. Paul Coyne and Michael Wang

Objectives

By the end of this chapter, the reader will be able to:

- Describe the terms and concepts pertaining to raising money, launching a product, and forming a business.

- Provide examples of strategies to raise capital and their impact to the original creator and founder.

- Reflect and articulate your true end goal, and determine the best course to achieve the end goal.

"Always deliver more than expected."

— Larry Page, cofounder, Google (Forbes.com, 2018)

At this point, you may have a great idea and are beginning to understand that it will take great deal of effort to turn this idea into a reality. You may also be realizing that no matter how great your idea is and how hard you focus your effort, you will need money to advance your idea. While this chapter focuses on funding and commercialization, it is extremely important that there remains a consistent recognition that all the money in the world cannot replace a good idea and your efforts.

Still, funding is necessary to advance your idea. The first step in the process of securing funding for an innovation/invention is to recognize that, much like your effort, sacrifice is also required. The first choice in the funding discussion is either to self-fund or to not self-fund the innovation. Either of these choices requires consideration and sacrifice. If self-funding is preferred, sacrifice will be needed in terms of your personal savings. If funding is sought outside yourself, sacrifice will be required in terms of relinquishing some control over decision making and shared financial return when/if the innovation becomes successful. There is no right or wrong way to make this decision or any of the other decisions outlined in this chapter. The only bad decision is one that comes from a lack of diligence and understanding on the part of the innovator. The only weapon in the fight against ignorance is knowledge.

The first thing to help you make the decision to self-fund or seek outside funding is to orient yourself as to who owns the intellectual property (IP). Intellectual property was discussed earlier and is very important to the funding conversation. Consider whether you are self-employed or employed as part of an organization that may claim the IP. If you are employed, you will need to arm yourself with the knowledge of your current employer's policy regarding the IP of their employees. For this, you will need an attorney to assist you. Take this very seriously as it *will* impact your future goals.

Who will own/owns the IP is extremely important to the funding conversation for this reason: if an innovator works for a company that has an IP policy in place, the decision to self-fund or not does not lie exclusively with the innovator. The employer is given the "right of first refusal" to be involved with the innovation/invention, and if an employee does not follow this process, the employer will most likely claim the right to the intellectual property when/if the invention becomes successful. The legal and ethical implications of these policies are widely debated, but regardless, this is the reality, and an innovator must know this and take steps to ensure protection. As stated in the previous chapter, always make sure that your employer's decision of whether to embark with you on the innovation journey is in writing; retain this document.

Most times, the employer will not opt to partner with the innovator, and even if they do, the employer will assist with patent search and filing, market research, and some joint marketing, but this is likely not an exhaustive list of expenses. After this potential variable in the decision-making process is accounted for, the innovator is yet again faced with the initial decision of whether to self-fund. One consideration is if the intent is to create a product or a company. To drill deeper on this, think about whether it is your intent to create a company that will produce, market, sell, and distribute your invention or to invent a product and then use other companies to facilitate this process, with you receiving royalties, or a portion of profit, for your invention. This latter model is called *licensing*.

> "I'm convinced that about half of what separates the successful entrepreneurs from the non-successful ones is pure perseverance."
>
> — Steve Jobs, cofounder and CEO, Apple (Forbes.com, 2018)

Startup

If you decide that you are going to start a business or company nowadays, this is known as a "startup." This is an important fact because knowing the language and terms will open doors to you as you proceed through the lengthy and trying process of advancing your work and building a business.

The differences between for profit or non-profit

The decision to determine what kind of company to set up is heavily influenced by how you wish to initially fund, and continue to fund, the company. Each type of company structure has its advantages and disadvantages, and it is important to understand the nature and the maintenance costs of each.

The first decision to consider is whether the company should be for-profit or non-profit. A common misconception is that non-profit corporations and companies don't make money and that their executives do not make a sustainable living or even "substantial" money. This could not be further from the truth. There are nearly three times as many non-profit hospitals as for-profit hospitals in the United States, and a simple internet search for the average salary for hospital CEO will show you that these individuals are doing quite well financially. So can you if you choose to go this route—the choice is yours.

The main advantage of a non-profit corporation is that when it raises money from other companies, those companies are able to deduct the amount given from their taxes, as the IRS views it as a charitable gift. If your invention is tied to a larger social cause, you may be eligible to create a non-profit around this cause and then place this "innovation/invention" within it. A non-profit is able to solicit donations from other companies and individuals (including you) in ways that a for-profit company cannot.

However, many individuals will not give substantial amounts of money as donations and will want to know, "What's in it for me?" with every dollar contributed. Creating a for-profit corporation gives a clearer answer to what to expect in return.

Types of company structures

There are three main types of companies to think about. These include a sole proprietorship, a partnership, and a corporation.

Sole proprietorship: This is the most simple. It is just you, the innovator/inventor, filing the paperwork and indicating that you are now doing business as "your company name."

Partnership: This model is slightly more involved. This is due to the fact that there are various partnership structure types and more than one person involved. However, there are many similarities to sole proprietorship.

Corporation: This is a distinct legal entity that can be owned by one or more individuals. These offer the most legal protection and tax benefits but are also costly to create and maintain. The most popular corporate structures regarding for-profit corporations are C-Corp, S-Corp, and LLC (limited liability company).

This is an overview, and you will need to do your own research about the advantages and disadvantages of each of these structures. Some make it easier to raise money fast, while others make it easier to raise money later or even to sell your company. Gain as much understanding as you can, and then start talking to attorneys. Most attorneys will have exploratory calls free of charge with potential clients. Call as many as you can, and tell them your unique situation of what you are trying to create. With their assistance, you can make an informed decision.

Call to action:

Take time each day, until you are comfortable, to watch internet videos about forming a business, listening to definitions and explanations of these terms and the lessons learned from other entrepreneurs. Seek out mentors who have gone through this before and can help educate you. Use this information to help you reach out to an attorney and make your own decisions.

With both a clear understanding of the involvement of your current employer (if you have one) and a decision surrounding the legal structure you will create for your innovation/invention, the decision around whether to self-fund is getting closer. The next step is to have an understanding of the true costs associated with starting this work. To start this process, map out all the costs that you think will be incurred in making this effort successful. Remember that no matter what you think, it will always cost more. Once you complete an assessment of the necessary costs to start up your innovation/invention or company, you are now ready to think through whether you want to self-fund.

To self-fund or not?

At this point, you will likely start telling people about your idea. There are legal steps to protect you during these conversations that were explained in the previous chapter, so be careful. When you open up about your idea, many people will ask if they can become involved. It is not uncommon for many people to want to be part of a great innovation at the time it is being discussed. Do not mistake this for them having the same passion as you. The stories of Steve Jobs, Amazon, and McDonald's have been so deeply ingrained in the psyche of the entire population that no one wants to "miss out" on their chance to catch a ride to riches. The same force that is propelling you to innovate lies within everyone, but the vast majority of the population are not willing to put in the effort it takes to become successful in this way. Seek people to be involved who will give their mind, their great effort, and their money. You will likely find very few who can, or desire to, give all three. So, whenever someone says, "Let me in!" ask yourself the following two questions: 1)"Which of the three things of mind, effort, and money can this person give?" and 2) "Does my innovation need it?"

This holds true for friends and family as well. Do not lower your guard—this is not Thanksgiving dinner, where all are welcome. Be extremely cautious about whom you take money from and whom you let into the inner circle of business. Not all friends make good business partners. Not all business partners make good friends. Before taking money from your family and friends, you have to be 100-percent certain that if all their money is lost, they will be okay with it, or your noble attempt at innovation will lead to a lifetime of very lonely Thanksgiving dinners.

"Trust your instincts."

— Estée Lauder, founder, Estée Lauder (Forbes.com, 2018)

Funding options

Self-funding

One funding option is to fund your innovation and business yourself. This process, known as self-funding, means that you invest your own money into the costs associated with the invention and business. If you have the financial resources to do this and the risks associated with the potential of losing the money you invested are acceptable to you, this may be a viable option. The benefit of this is that you maintain 100-percent ownership of the invention, as well as the company, and therefore stand to gain 100 percent of the profits. You also may qualify for small business loans, from either the government or the bank, to lessen the amount of upfront capital (investment) needed. Be very cautious when borrowing money, as you will need to pay it back, regardless of how successful your business is.

There are many other options to weigh outside of self-funding and taking money from friends and family. None of these choices are mutually exclusive, so you are free to choose one, a few, or even all these options.

Crowdfunding/Crowdsourcing

The internet has brought about a new way to raise money, known as crowdfunding. Crowdfunding is exactly what it sounds like. You wish to raise money and so ask a crowd to fund it. There are now hundreds of internet platforms that facilitate crowdfunding. Typically, the public is exposed to crowdfunding in the form of donation websites, such as the popular GoFundMe. An example of this may be that someone you know is diagnosed with a serious disease or has a death in the family, and one of their family members or friends sets up a "page" for people (anyone) to donate money to help out and posts it on social media. Raising money through crowdsourcing is that easy. Except in the case of a startup, it is not a donation, but rather an investment.

What many people do not realize is that the majority of these crowdfunding websites take 3-10 percent of all money given. Meaning that if you donate $100 to your good friend in their time of need, you may actually be giving between $90 to $97 to your friend and $3-7 dollars to the crowdsourcing platform (this is their business model).

Crowdsourcing may be an acceptable arrangement on a small scale, but if you are raising $500,000 to start a company and keeping only $475,000, you have essentially paid $25,000 to use the crowdsourcing platform. You may decide that this is worth it because the platform provided the "vehicle" by which you raised $500,000. Consider, however, that if you could have raised the $500,000 without the platform, you just paid $25,000 for no reason at all.

Much of these crowdsourcing platforms for ideas and products are modeled, with slight variations, after the popular Kickstarter. Unlike in donation crowdsourcing platforms, the "funders" are promised money in exchange for something, typically the product, and their credit cards are charged only when the goal is reached, to ensure that the goal needed to achieve success is met before money is given. This is often known as the "terms" for the investors.

Here is another example: if your goal is to raise $100,000 for your sister because she is having surgery, and you only receive $50,000 in donations, your sister will get $50,000, minus platform fees (3-10 percent). However, if you seek to create a revolutionary new cane for the elderly and need raise $100,000 to meet your goal but only raise $50,000 by the deadline, the individuals who funded the amount will not have their credit cards charged. Since you didn't meet your goal of $100,000, you would not receive the money for your project. This is because there was not enough money raised to ensure that the individuals who pre-ordered canes can get them.

These crowdfunding platforms for product ideas are designed to allow you, the owner/producer, as well as the public who seeks to buy the newly created product, to benefit from what is known as "economy of scale." The definition of an economy of scale is a decrease in cost gained by an increase in production (Corporatefinanceinstitute.com, 2019). An example of this is when you buy a ten-pack of paper towels because the cost per roll is significantly less than buying the smaller two-pack. In this case, you are realizing the benefit of economies of scale at the consumer level. Crowdfunding websites allow you to realize the benefit of economy of scale at the production level and pass this on to the consumers who are signing up early and promising to purchase your newly created good.

Equity crowdfunding

When creating a company, money can be raised in a similar way, in the form of "equity crowdfunding." Instead of raising money by promising the consumer your new product, you raise money by promising a portion of perpetual profit from your product in the form of equity. In equity crowdsourcing, a valuation is set on how much your company is worth. This is posted on an equity crowdfunding platform, and ideally, other people think your company is worth that as well. If they agree and think your company has potential, they can, and often will, invest.

Dilution

Dilution is when you will only own a predetermined percentage of the company and the profits that are left over after expenses, and you distribute shares. This happens when money is raised in the form of equity, whether from an equity crowdfunding platform or through a traditional legal contract. Here is an example: consider that the company is valued at $900,000 and you raise $100,000. The company is now worth $1,000,000 (because it was worth $900,000 before and now has $100,000 in the bank). You now own 90 percent of the company because 10 percent of the ownership has gone to the new investment partners who invested $100,000.

Skill-building exercise:

> Flip to a blank page. Draw a circle. Divide the circle into various sized slices of how you wish to divide ownership of your idea, sort of like a pizza. Now, draw a bigger circle than your first circle. Cut out your original circle and pick it up and place it inside the larger circle. Notice how the original proportions of the first circle have not changed, but they no longer make up the entire circle. This exercise represents dilution.

The most important part of this exercise is how the new circle increased in size. You have less of a percentage of the new circle compared to the first, but the circle itself is bigger. It is that simple. Your company is worth more—you don't own as much of this company percentage wise, but the cash value of what you do own has increased.

To express the concept of dilution in mathematical terms, take the following example: You had an idea and realized that you needed help to grow it, so you gave a business partner 50 percent of the business because without them, the business could not grow. You now own 50 percent of your business. Someone then comes along and says they will give you $5 million for half of your company. This means that the entire business is now worth $10 million. You owned 50 percent of the business before agreeing to the deal. Once that business "pie" increases again, you will own 50 percent of 50 percent, or 25 percent. This equals $2.5 million. Would you rather have 50 percent of your and your business partner's idea or $2.5 million? As you can see, dilution is not always a negative thing. In fact, it is often a necessary byproduct of growth.

That being said, while it is simple philosophically, legal contracts are not simple at all. This is where you will certainly need an attorney. Do not be so focused on percentages that you are afraid to grow your business. An important caveat to note is that at some point, when you no longer own 50 percent or more of the voting shares of a company, you will no longer have control of the company. This is why some early founders issue convertible notes as opposed to giving up equity to investors immediately.

Convertible notes

A convertible note is a debt instrument (tool) that accrues interest and converts to stock upon hitting a future predetermined milestone, such as raising a significant amount of money. A convertible note simply states that the company promises to pay the noteholders back with interest in the future, in the form of cash or equity, depending on the nature of the note, and does not mean that the noteholder is a current owner of the company. Issuing convertible notes is one way to potentially remain holding majority control for a longer period of time as your business gets off the ground, while still being able to raise money because the outcome takes effect in the future.

Sweat equity

This is the value placed on your own time and effort that is/has been placed in the development, growth, and advancement of the business. This holds real monetary value and should be treated as a cash equivalent. Whenever you raise money from other people, no matter the vehicle, do not forget to account for this time and effort. The saying, "time is money," is especially true for entrepreneurs.

This chapter is meant to provide a basic introduction into equity dealings and is by no means comprehensive. Most of the time, it is not this simple, and if you are dealing with sophisticated investors, they will likely use that to their advantage and attempt to place complex structures in contracts that you may not understand and will not work to your benefit. If you do not understand something, ask your attorney. It is important that you read every contract, as well as have your attorney review every contract before you sign. This may seem daunting and overwhelming; however, you are a nurse and can critically think your way through it. You have handled far greater and more difficult challenges, both intellectually and emotionally, than informing yourself about business dealings.

Incubators/Accelerators

Another option to help get your innovation/invention off the ground is to apply for an incubator or an accelerator program. Many individuals use these terms interchangeably, but they are not the same. As nurses, we know that an incubator is used at the earliest stages of life to help a baby grow alongside other growing babies. A business incubator is the same thing. If you and your invention are chosen for an incubator, your new company is placed with other new companies and given resources, connections, and potentially, funding to help it grow in exchange for some modest equity.

Involvement in an accelerator involves much of the same structure but occurs when a company has increased the likelihood that it can survive and wishes to take steps to accelerate its growth. This can even be after an incubator. Make sure to do extensive research before joining an incubator or accelerator. Do not assume that because you and your innovation/idea are selected, you should immediately join. You will quickly learn that as an entrepreneur, there are pros and cons to every decision.

"Free" money

The best kind of money is free money. It doesn't happen often but it does exist. Be aware that most of the opportunities that claim to provide "free" money for innovation awards will come with many obligations that are in the fine print—some even include partial ownership in your product. Make sure you read everything very carefully (always a good idea to have an attorney review in advance). The United States government (and other governments as well) have grants that you can find online. The process of applying for a grant is cumbersome and typically requires paying someone who is skilled in formal grant writing. Many of these individuals have introductory calls free of charge, so do not hesitate to find Small Business Association (SBA) or Small Business Innovation Research (SBIR)/Small Business Technology Transfer (STTR) grant writers online and call them to educate yourself about the process.

In addition, more and more companies are beginning to view nurses as an untapped source of knowledge for innovative ideas and business opportunities. Many grants, awards, and pitch competitions are being sponsored and subsidized by these corporate partners in an effort to learn about their ideas, discover potentially new companies in which to invest, and at a minimum, provide great PR, as everyone loves it when nurses are rewarded. Provided that you are comfortable with the fine print, these kinds of opportunities are great exposure for your idea, and the incremental wins can add up.

Call to action:

Search the internet for awards, grants, pitch competitions, accelerators, and incubators to see which may be applicable to you. Read through the criteria. Do you meet them? What is the application process? Start it and see how far you get. If it is within your reach or a good stretch goal, submit it.

The real question is not about how much of the company you own, but rather how much of what you do own is worth. A deeper question is, how much does the answer to the previous question factor into the reasons you are doing this in the first place? Again, back to motivation, which is why we started this book on the subject. If the answer is that money is the only reason you are doing this, then becoming an entrepreneur isn't for you.

While you are raising capital, building a team, and getting your product or solution ready for market, it is extremely important to remember that the healthcare sales cycle is notoriously long. From the beginning, a clear path to market must be planned. It is best to start this process as early as possible.

Minimum viable product

The typical path is to raise enough money to create a minimum viable product, or MVP. This is the most minimal creation that allows your product to function, albeit in a rudimentary and maybe "not so pretty" way. The creation of an MVP or tangible good serves three purposes.

* First, it shows you if what you created is indeed a viable and working product.

* Second, future investors are able to see that you have something for them to invest in and that it is more than a nicely designed presentation.

* Third, potential clients or buyers of your product or solution can give you feedback about what improvements would be needed in order for them to purchase the product.

Commercializing

Commercialization encompasses all the steps that are required to bring your innovation to market. It actually begins the moment you have an idea. Right then, you should be thinking of the steps that must be taken before your innovation is available for public use.

Prototyping, or the creation of a minimum viable product and subsequent prototypes of increasing complexity, is the process of creating an innovation produced in a singular quantity to demonstrate efficacy and for testing to determine further developmental paths. Once a prototype is deemed viable, the next step is to determine how to manufacture it in a cost-effective way with the goal of producing multiple high-quality products. This process can have multiple steps, depending on the complexity of your innovation. At a minimum, it involves fabrication, assembly, and packaging. Fabrication is the process of selecting the individual components that will make up your larger solution and putting them together. This could be as simple as selecting the wood that will be turned into a walking stick and sawing it for your height or as complex as determining all the components that make up a motor vehicle and creating a factory to effectively produce each part. Assembly is the process of putting the fabricated parts together for the desired final product. Packaging is the process of safely wrapping them and arranging them to look attractive for sale.

Call to action:

> Search for "rapid prototyping" businesses in your area. Meet with as many of these businesses as possible to discuss prototyping your idea. Be very careful whom you select to work with. Don't jump at the cheapest one without asking questions first. Ask to speak with references or the companies for whom this business has produced prototypes. As with most things, you get what you pay for.

Once you have your product, the next step in the commercialization process is to sell it. In healthcare, it is extremely important that you remember that the sales cycle, or the time it takes to sell a product, is notoriously long. Innovation and entrepreneurship is not a baseball diamond, where you go to first base, then second, then third, and then home. You must be at each place in your mind and in your action, simultaneously fluidly moving back and forth as your innovation evolves. This is especially true in the healthcare sales cycle. Do not wait until you have the finished product to begin having conversations with decision makers in hospitals and healthcare. This must be done concurrently, both for iterative feedback and so you do not have to wait years following the completion of your product to see adoption.

After your innovation/invention or business gains traction, you will find that there are three kinds of people in the world with regard to understanding entrepreneurs and startups. The first group includes many individuals, especially those with limited understanding, who see you as a successful businessperson and think, "Wow, they must be rich!" The second group, who knows a little bit more about dilution, raising capital, and has a basic understanding of the process, will say, "How much of the company do you still own?" The third group is reserved for those who have directly observed the process, either by being an entrepreneur themselves or by witnessing a loved one be an entrepreneur, and they will simply say, "Great job." That is a true compliment!

> "You miss 100 percent of the shots that you don't take."

> — Wayne Gretzky (BrainyQuote, 2019)

The most important differentiator you have in becoming an innovator, entrepreneur, or business owner is that you are a nurse. This is a superpower. Use it to your advantage. You are part of the most trusted profession in the world. Your career is helping other people. If you call up and say, "Hi, I am a nurse, and I was hoping to ask for thirty minutes of your time to get your opinion on how to improve a new solution we are creating for patient care," you will be very surprised how many people are willing to speak to you. As with anything, without trying, the answer will always be zero. So, just try! You will doubt yourself many times along the way, just as we all have, and when you do, try anyway. Keep going and ultimately, you will succeed.

References

BrainyQuote.com (2019). Wayne Gretzky. Retrieved on March 13, 2019. Retrieved from https://www.brainyquote.com/authors/wayne_gretzky.

Corporatefinanceinstitute.com. (2019). Accessed on March 19, 2019. Accessed at https://corporatefinanceinstitute.com/resources/knowledge/economics/economies-of-scale/.

Forbes.com. (2018). Larry Page quote. Retrieved on March 18, 2019. Retrieved at https://www.forbes.com/sites/allbusiness/2014/02/10/50-inspirational-quotes-for-startups-and-entrepreneurs/#30eb57646ef0.

Forbes.com. (2018). Estee Lauder quote. Retrieved on March 18, 2019. Retrieved at https://www.forbes.com/sites/allbusiness/2014/02/10/50-inspirational-quotes-for-startups-and-entrepreneurs/#30eb57646ef0.

Forbes.com. (2018). Steve Jobs quote. Retrieved on March 18, 2019. Retrieved at https://www.forbes.com/sites/allbusiness/2014/02/10/50-inspirational-quotes-for-startups-and-entrepreneurs/#30eb57646ef0.

7 Marketing and Promotion

By Vince Baiera

Objectives:

By the end of this chapter, the reader will be able to:

- Explain the target market.
- Identify the best practices for content development.
- Design a marketing strategy to highlight the key venture/product.

"The best marketing doesn't feel like marketing."

— Tom Fishburne (blog.wishpond.com, 2019)

Creating a new product or starting a company is one thing; telling the world it exists is another. Telling your story in this crowded, loud world is not easy to do, but doing it well is the difference between your new business/product having a chance to succeed and your new business/product failing. This concept starts with a basic idea that will drive every decision necessary to successfully market your product. Think of it as a simple equation: marketing equals attention. Good marketing is grabbing people's attention and getting people to talk about your product and share your message. Ongoing branding is the overall message you convey through your marketing.

Have you ever heard about a scandal and the people in the media saying, "This is a PR nightmare!" This means that the *attention* that the company is receiving is *bad* attention (versus *good* attention). Realizing that every effort you make to tell the world about your product or business is, in fact, marketing will help keep you focused on the overall goal.

Real-world example:

I'll be sharing lessons I learned while launching the step2bed™ to illustrate best practices and pitfalls to avoid. Pay close attention to even the smallest of details that will help you navigate the marketing and promotion process. The step2bed™ is designed to help seniors or people with mobility disorders get in and out of bed safely and reduce their risk of falls. My grandparents were the inspiration for this product, and my seven years as an ICU nurse helped me create the best product I could for older adults. As the product took form and was ready to be manufactured, the focus shifted to creating a marketing plan to tell the world that this product existed.

Great work takes time!

Do not wait until two weeks before you want to launch your product to develop the marketing plan and content. The secret most people don't understand is that the messaging, videos, articles, and posts made by successful brands are created months in advance and are pre-scheduled to generate optimal results. I started about four to five months before my product was ready to sell because I knew this and didn't want to be unprepared.

Developing the marketing plan, deciding what to create (articles, videos, images, posts), and identifying the target market will probably take a week or two. Once you determine how you are going to communicate, experts may be needed to help with graphic design, artwork, voice-over, etc. Identifying professionals to create the content you need will probably take another week. By the time the start dates are scheduled and content is refined, plan for another two to four weeks to go by. During this time, scripts are written and your marketing messages are refined. Finally, the "big day" of video shooting or recording arrives—what's next? There will likely be another two to five weeks for content editing and review. You will typically identify things that need adjustments, which will take another two to three weeks before it is ready to go. In total, around six to eight weeks are spent on this, and that is if everything goes right. The first time through this process, everything takes much longer than expected. Things like writer's block, getting side-tracked with life, timelines, or commitments not being honored, or running out of cash can all impact the deliverables and timelines. Assume in advance that it will take longer than you think, so it's important to budget enough time and money.

The timeline has been mapped out to prepare the content and it is time to begin, but how? For step2bed™, six videos were created for the product launch, and that number actually grew to more than ten because videos were created in several languages for a "global launch." The overview video designed to sell directly to seniors would be the main video created for the website and marketing purposes. Another video was created to market to potential customers with knee or hip issues and physical therapy patients. Additionally, an assembly video was made to supplement the assembly instructions, and then finally, an infomercial was made. The infomercial was meant to educate the customer and at the end, inform them that they could buy the product. Finally, short, one-minute-long general content videos were made so they could be posted on various social media platforms. In total, almost forty videos were made to set up the first six months of the product launch, to be used on different platforms to promote the product, educate the audience, and capture the *attention* of consumers. This all started by studying basic copywriting principles that would help create clean copy that would educate the market and simplify the message. The four longer main videos required writing, editing, modifying, and re-writing of the intended messaging. The general education videos were intended to add value, which required the researching of topics that would resonate with the target market or ideal audience.

It took five days of recording to get all the videos completed and then approximately six to eight weeks to complete the editing, and it was well worth it! By the time the products arrived, the professional-looking marketing videos were ready to tell the story. The videos were used to develop partnerships, market the product, and drive sales. The general education videos were used to build a following and put a face to the company—important because the product was developed by a nurse for seniors—and they provided a way to help people build trust with the product.

The overall plan worked because there were stockpiles of videos with great content that were slowly pushed out day by day to keep the *attention* of followers and build engagement. The ability to continually create great posts that are thought-provoking gives you the complementary ability to educate the audience about things *they* care about. Creating engagement means adding value by sharing great tips and articles and creating thought-provoking posts to generate interest and get people talking. Eventually, this creates a relationship where the customer views the product and/or company as one that provides value and is not just selling a product. The customers trust that their best interests are at heart and reciprocate by engaging through social media. When reminded about the step2bed™ product, customers were more open to purchasing it for themselves or a loved one since we had already created a "relationship."

I wish I could tell you that the first day you launch your product or idea, you'll get a worldwide response and people will flock to your site to buy what you are selling. Very few companies "take off" like that and have overnight success, and if they do, it's because they have a great idea and (usually) the financial backing that allows them to market.

> *"A journey of a thousand miles starts with one single step."*

> —Lao Tzu (Nash & Jang. 2015)

Along the way, I have identified best practices to build awareness and drive sales. These are simple things that can begin as the product is taking shape and will help prepare you for the product/service launch. Keep in mind that you will be constantly challenged to do things that you *think* are above your ability and skill level. You may even have second thoughts about whether anyone will want to buy what you're selling or if you have made a big mistake. Whenever you are having those fears, remember one thing that has helped me tremendously over the years: "Don't be afraid to do something you're not qualified to do" (Carlin 2017).

If you have decided to create a product and sell it to the world to make a positive impact on people's lives, then get started. Don't wait for someone to tell you that you *should* do it or that you *could* do it; simply make a decision and get started.

Call to action

> Identify two to three people/companies you follow/admire that sell something (a product or service), and review their social media pages. You may also have to visit their site and even review their blog. Review the last three to four months of their pages, and write down the answers to the following questions. Now look for the patterns that emerge.

- How often do they put out content?

- How often do they make a post about the product that they are selling?

- How do they do it?

- Is it direct and interactive?

- Is it through thought-provoking articles or questions?

- Do they use someone famous to sell their products or tell stories?

- Do you follow this person or company on more than one platform?

- If they sent you a message through a social media network, would you feel special or obligated to respond?

Don't make marketing too complicated

Most likely, these are big companies or famous/rich people who are selling something, and they have the money to invest in marketing professionals to help them build their brand. Remember, they are spending tens or hundreds of thousands, if not millions, to keep your *attention* so eventually, you will buy something from them. *The key is to model what they are doing so you can have similar results in a much cheaper way.*

Think about how simple this is: it is not rocket science and it is not hard, it just takes an understanding of what your goals are and the discipline to stick to a timeline to get started. When examining the companies/individuals that I admired and wanted to model, I started to look at how I could make content to rival what they are doing. I decided to create videos as my main strategy since they are more interactive and create energy when communicating the message. Your preference may be writing blog posts, taking photos, or making videos. Start to think about how and where you want to tell your story, and get started.

Who is the target market? Are you selling to adults, children, working professionals, mothers, etc.? On what platforms and sites are they spending time where you could compete for their *attention?* Maybe you've created a product for healthcare professionals to make their job easier? Where are healthcare professionals spending time and consuming content? Are they active on healthcare blogs? What about professional organizations like the American Nursing Association? The bottom line is that you will need to do research to find your answer and start to cross-reference what you want to create, and identify the best medium to deliver that content.

Target Market

If you are not sure who your target audience is, start here to refine this until you have an answer. Focus on the target market with demographics such as age (e.g., ten-year-olds) or age cohort (e.g., college students), gender, profession, pet owners, people with medical conditions, etc. Spend quality time doing online searches to help you develop the correct target market. For the step2bed™, adult children between the ages of forty-five and sixty-five were identified as the target market, which was determined after reading the reviews of other senior products and learning who actually purchased such products. Patterns emerged, with older adults saying that they were buying that product for their aging parents. This was confirmation that adult children were the right customers that step2bed™ would end up targeting.

Using Social Media Channels

Next, consider what platforms or social media channels that this audience is using: Facebook, Instagram, LinkedIn, Twitter, Snapchat, Pinterest, etc. Are there other platforms where this audience could be reached? Doing research to find those answers will save you a great deal of time in the long run. For step2bed™, Facebook and Instagram were used as the main marketing channels due to the fact that this would reach the most people and they were platforms I felt comfortable on.

From there, cross-reference the platforms you want to use with the type and frequency of content you want to create. In my case, short one-minute videos (Instagram videos can only be one minute in length), thought-provoking images, and quotes could educate my market. Pictures with short captions could be pushed out to Twitter easily to capture a larger audience. If you pay attention to step2bed™ videos and messaging, it is all targeted to the audience that is the buyer of my product: adult children looking for products for aging parents.

Start your post with attention-grabbing questions, such as; "Is your mom or dad struggling with mobility? If so, this message is for you!" All the messaging is congruent to speak to the target audience and continue to gain market share. If the target market is not identified as the key market to sell the product, then the appropriate content cannot be created. Remember, creating copy for the content is a difficult skill that takes time and practice to master and is key to generating revenue. For example, half of the content can't "speak" to one group of people and the other half "speak" to another. Be crystal clear on whom you are marketing to and how your product/service can improve their life.

Call to action

Identify the social media platforms you wish to use, and create a page/site for your product or service. If it's a blog page, then consider buying the domain (URL) you wish to use to start your blog (also discussed in chapter three). You can download the apps through the app store or start a page using the business pages of the apps you're using. If you need to buy a domain, there are many sites out there to buy from, such as GoDaddy.com, HostGator.com, or Domains.com. Start by securing a site or writing content and posting on an existing blog. The point is to just start.

To optimize your social media footprint, take a look at a program called Hootsuite (hootsuite.com). This program ties together all social media apps in one central place and allows you to schedule the release of content. Hootsuite has a small per-month cost, but it saves a great deal of time and allows you to make one message and post it on three different sites, even coordinating the times so it's automated to make the biggest impact. Remember that most of the content you see from companies and individuals has been developed and scheduled months in advance. Using programs such as this for two to five hours/month will allow you to plan and drip-feed content around a monthly marketing calendar to optimize results. In just one afternoon, a monthly social media campaign can be created to help you maintain a constant presence for your customers, without actually having to spend time on it every single day.

This is how successful marketers and companies post their content in order to make sure they are efficient and effective in their approach. If you are like Gary Vaynerchuk and spend $3 million a year on promotion and marketing and have a staff of eighteen people who coordinate and push out daily content for you, then by all means, do it! If you're just like everyone else in the world, on a tight budget and with only yourself to develop content, use this strategy and it can be effective.

In the example for step2bed™, I wanted to educate the market and create thought-provoking images and quotes to remind them that my product exists and is, in fact, available for sale. In order to feel comfortable doing this, I needed to have a long-term vision and be consistent with my approach. I broke the marketing strategy into tactics of six posts per week and focused on education, not just sell, sell, sell. Two days a week would be dedicated to educational content such as the one-minute videos created for "health tips" or ways to avoid falls by modifying the customer's home so they could safely age-in-place. Two days a week included photos to remind people that falls do happen and that if they aren't taking preventative measures, their loved one could have a fall injury. Photos were interchanged with people comfortably aging-in-place and potential fall environments, to help them realize that prevention is the best way to help achieve their long-term desired outcome, which is aging in their own home. Finally, two posts per week showed a photo of the step2bed™, a video testimonial, or a video clip of the product to remind them that there is a real-world solution. Consistency is important, so most weeks are the same from a marketing perspective because the long-term result will build a loyal group of followers who truly connect with the brand and our mission. They will gain value along the way and eventually be ready to buy a step2bed™, and those short videos or photos of our great product will activate them at just the right time.

Let's fast forward and pretend that you have identified your target market, acquired a domain, and checked out which platforms to use and are starting to feel confident about what you can accomplish. You have a plan, you have ideas on how to create content to help reach your audience, and you have topics you want to work on that might even generate a response from your audience. Make sure you have given yourself plenty of time to create the content and ensure that you are operating efficiently, so you are not wasting time and money along the way.

When thinking about great content, it is important to remember that it is likely going to come in one of three forms: written, video, or visual images. When starting out, you may only have a smartphone to record videos or take photos, which will work, although it is best to use a professional camera or video recorder. If you are writing, make sure it is edited and proofread because grammatical errors can ruin your credibility. Today, there are so many programs, devices, camera lenses, and tools to help you make great content, it is worth investing a little bit so your content looks top-notch.

"Good content is the best SEO."

— Robert Scoble (Ferriss 2016).

Good content is everything! It's more important than a fancy logo, header, or intro to your video. It's more important than a professional video with perfect editing. If you can have someone edit the videos or record them on a professional camera, they will be better. However, it isn't the end of the world if this is not possible. Being authentic and being yourself is key because if you are trying to "sell" something, people will see right through that. Be yourself, stick to what you are good at, and don't try to be the replica of someone else. In fact, you won't pull it off, so instead, be yourself and be unique to create your own "lane" in the market.

Think about how your video content or images can look as great as possible. Think about the camera you are going to use or where you can get one. Does a friend of yours own one that would work perfectly for you? Would you be able to talk with them and ask if they could help you? Maybe you could trade services? What if your friend could help you record and even edit, and you offer something of value to them in return? Maybe you tutor their child, mow their lawn, etc. The point is that if you are creative, find a good camera that you can use. Be sure to check for this too: if the content is ready to record, will it take one or two sittings?

There are companies that will rent high-end camera equipment by the day, and depending on your location, this may prove to be expensive. You can rent a tripod, a camera, lenses, and more per day and record everything over a long weekend. You may have to ask your friends about what to rent and what would work best for what you're looking to develop. From there, ask if they can offer their advice on how to do it and what tips they can give. Throughout the process, you'll be surprised at how many people will want to help you, since you're going out on a limb and doing something different through your business.

Finding help with business tasks

Getting help with services is easy these days. Ask your friends on Facebook who is good at video editing and reasonably priced. Inquire about their skill level, quality of work, and if they would be willing to help your business goals on a budget. Maybe you can find a videographer cheap if you tell them that you will use the videos in a global campaign and give them credit for the videography work. Explain that if they help you here, you will help them with something in the future—it can't hurt to see what they say. In general, utilize your network to see if someone can help you for cheap.

Another secret that is often forgotten or overlooked is using interns. College interns from your local community college or university are working to build their skills and get real-world experience with a product or company to help them build their resume. Your product/service would provide them with the experience of a new product/service that is cutting edge and useful for people around the world. In return, you will receive a young, hungry student who is probably better at what you need than you are and willing to help you for cheap or maybe even for free.

There are incredibly bright students from around the world who attend the local colleges and universities, and if your business applies to the college as a business partner, this allows you to hire students to work on eight- to twelve-week internships to complete projects. Interns can be utilized for building a new website, creating videos for a marketing launch, creating a new logo or sell sheet, or laying out a social media plan. The point is, you are able to offer these inexperienced, albeit smart, people a great chance to help you without breaking the bank. Some roles are unpaid, while some are paid. If the market value to do your work is $1,000, you can most likely find a college kid to help you do it for $200. Be fair, be kind, and add value by offering to write letters of recommendation or allowing them to showcase their work as part of their portfolio or on social media platforms. Teach and mentor them along the way with the skills and approaches that you know will help them when they graduate and enter the real world. This means giving clear directions and helping them develop a project timeline for the work they are doing and providing them constructive feedback along the way.

Craigslist is another place to seek out qualified part-time talent looking to make extra cash in their spare time or freelancers looking for "work for hire." You can create an ad for the work that you need completed, and people in your area will inquire and can be hired by you. With patience, finding qualified people for occasional work will help you build a network so you can outsource jobs to people whose work you are already familiar with. One example from my own company is that I recently started adding handwritten "thank you" cards to every step2bed™ unit that shipped. I didn't want to personally write more than 1,000 handwritten cards since it isn't the best use of my time, so I created a listing on Craigslist, and within about thirty minutes, there were twenty people who applied for the job.

One rule to remember when you're working with interns or other paid talent for hire: You can *never* be too clear or specific in your direction. Remember that other people can't read your mind, and although you may think you're adequately explaining what needs to be done, it most likely can be explained even more clearly. This will save you time, headache, and money along the way. Start with a clear job posting and expectations. After this is typed out, go back and re-read it at least two to three times. Think about ways you can be more clear and explain further what you want done. Ask a friend or spouse to read it and explain back what they think you're asking. You will quickly learn that you are not as clear as you think you are and that you can have even more clarity around certain points. This was one of my mistakes early on that I wish I would have been better at.

When it comes to the work that someone else will do for your product/company, be very specific in your instructions: Do you want a white background with blue lettering or white lettering on a blue background? How big should the lettering be? What type of font do you want? Do you want music in your videos? What song? How long does it play? Do you want a fade in or out for the video editing? Do you want a certain filter or graphics to show as the video plays? The moral of the story is to be specific and clear in your instructions so the job is completed the right way the first time. This will prevent someone working on a project for weeks, only for you to find out after they submit their final work that they didn't come close to what you wanted. It took a few rounds of interns to help me understand that I wasn't communicating effectively in asking them to accomplish the work that I needed done.

Another tip is to ask interns or work-for-hire contractors to perform a few steps of the work that you are asking of them and have them submit it for your review. This will allow you to check what they are doing and give additional direction if it's necessary to help them adapt to your specific taste/approach. I learned this the hard way with my first couple of projects because I waited until the work was completed and then realized that I should have checked it along the way.

There are also other options to find freelancers for your work-for-hire projects, such as Fiverr (fiverr.com), where work starts at $5 for a simple task to help you complete small projects. On Fiverr, you can hire graphic designers, videographers, copywriters, and other experts to help you along the way. If you are not comfortable writing a sales pitch, these sites can provide someone to write it for you. If you need to find a videographer in your area, Fiverr can help. Maybe you want to hire someone to write blog posts about certain subjects. Fiverr has great talent from around the world that can help you with your project, and their fees start at just $5 for a project. Prices increase as you hire better talent, while very good creative work can be done for under $20.

After the content is completed, it will require editing. If you are hiring a videographer, ask about their editing services. Editing happens prior to the posting of any content. If your content has incomplete sentences or misspelled words, you are going to lose credibility with your audience. It will appear as though you are not professional or even intelligent. You have worked hard to create a product or service that adds value to your consumer, so be sure the message is conveyed clearly. Trust yourself and your team, but verify all the work that is done so it's 100-percent ready to go.

Make the content as convenient for your readers/followers to "consume" as possible. For video content, you can use sites like Rev (rev.com) and Trint (trint.com) to transcribe the content or add captions that will keep followers engaged. Consider this: the target market will often be scrolling through their social media feeds during work hours and won't have the volume on. However, they can see/read the words if captions accompany your videos. This will help your content rank higher on YouTube or other platforms and become more searchable, since your words are transcribed. This feature is less expensive than it seems, often $1 per minute of video content. For the forty videos that I made, all of which were one minute in length, this would have cost $40 and would have improved the search results as the content was pushed out to the market.

Videos as a marketing tool

Earlier in the chapter, I said that I wanted to make an overview video, as well as a video for physical therapy patients that would tell our story. As much as I like the sound of my own voice, I didn't think it would get us the results that I wanted, so I knew I needed to hire a professional. The websites, Voice123.com and Voices.com, are sites where voice-over talent can be hired to give videos a professional sound and feel. The copy needs to be written as a script that the voice-over professional will read.

Before hiring voice-over talent, a job will need to be created on these sites to allow you to identify the best talent for the project. The job posting will let candidates to submit their voice reading of the script so you can choose whom you want. This will allow you to narrow down the voice and sound you want and get a voice-over professional for cheap rates.

In my example, the product is for seniors, and the marketing is to adult children buying for their older parents. It wouldn't be effective or credible if a teenager or young person was pitching the product. It needed to be someone between forty and sixty who had a commanding voice that sounded caring, energetic, and informative. I didn't want someone who sounded like a salesperson. Posting exactly what I needed with specific directions didn't take very long, and soon, qualified voice-over professionals started rolling in. Within a day, there were eighty people who submitted their reading of the script. After reviewing all these unique voice-over readings, a clear winner rose to the top. It was the person who met all the needs that were identified in advance and would get through to the target market. After clarifying the timeline and fee, the voice-over professional started the project, and it was completed within 24 hours.

From there, the voice-over recording was given to the videographer, who in turn, created the video to match up to the timing of the spoken words. This process allowed for a professional-sounding video with great images and video clips for the price tag of a couple hundred dollars, compared to a professional studio that would have cost thousands of dollars. Here is a secret that the big companies never want you to know: they use the same voice-over sites to recruit and hire talent as small business owners. This is another example of how finding out what the professionals are doing and modeling their behavior can save you a lot of money along the way.

Let's shift from videos and images to writing blogs and the impact they make on your readers/consumers and how that can help build your brand. Telling a story and being original is something that will connect you with your audience. One powerful way to do this is to be vulnerable. Are you nervous about writing blog posts? Tell your followers in the first blog post that you want to make a positive impact in the world and you are new at this and would like them to be gentle and "take it easy" on you. Are you concerned that you may offend someone with your ideas? Tell them that you know it might offend some of your readers, but it is an important point to make.

Remember, the best art divides the audience. If you write something that is safe and plain, then no one is going to remember it, and more importantly, you won't keep people's *attention*, which means they won't keep reading your posts in the future. Be yourself, have fun, make mistakes, and take chances. The followers will see that you are being authentic and that your values are in the right place. They will agree with you along the way about what you are sharing, and this will spread the word organically. This can be one of the scariest parts of marketing because inevitably, you will make someone mad and they will stop following. A lost follower means that they will never buy from you and you will lose that potential sale, which is the exact opposite of what you're going for. So, why do it?

If you don't position yourself as a bold thought leader, then half the people who would be your biggest fans and evangelists will also never buy from you. They will never share your message with their network and will never tell their friends to check you out because you will be plain, boring, and safe. You will have everyone say that you are average, and no one will be enthused about what you are saying or doing. Be bold, take chances, write about difficult things, and take a stance that you believe in and can clearly articulate. Do not be mean and hateful or coax people into doing unlawful or unsafe things.

If you have decided that writing a blog is the form of communication your market will engage with, it is time to get started. Large companies have staff who have perfected their craft, so they can write something that will get their target market to buy their product. This is likely who you are competing with, so perfecting the message is important. Read the books, *The Ultimate Sales Letter*, by Dan Kennedy, and *The Adweek Copywriting Handbook*, by Joseph Sugarman, to get a better idea of how you can write great copy that will help you sell your product or service. These are two great reads to learn more about how to write copy. They will give you simple tricks and tools to improve your messaging.

Case Study

Here is a great example of marketing a product: the Squatty Potty.™ The Squatty Potty™ took the world by storm when the Harmon Brothers were tasked to tell the story of a product that is used in the bathroom to have more effective bowel movements. It's a consumer product that is purchased by the end consumer, and tens of millions of units have been sold over the past couple of years. They use humor to discuss this otherwise unpleasant necessity of daily living—that is, taking a poop. Their commercial went viral and got more than fifty million views in total.

Take five minutes to watch it for yourself: https://www.youtube.com/watch?v=YbYWhdLO43Q (or visit YouTube and type in, "Squatty Potty™ Commercial").

Right now, you're probably laughing at this creative approach to telling a story and how much thought went into the advertising commercial. This is a great example of using comedy in an ad, and while it's done brilliantly, it's not without risk. Using comedy in advertising is very hard to do, and you can walk a fine line between coming across funny and endearing and saying/doing something offensive.

The Squatty Potty™ video uses known psychological triggers that are common in marketing and effective. Here is the breakdown from a marketing standpoint.

Step 1 — Get attention

Example: *"This is where your ice cream comes from. The creamy poop of a mystic unicorn. Totally clean, totally cool, and soft served straight from a sphincter."*

The goal is to get your audience's attention and "hook" them so they are intrigued enough to keep watching. A big promise, a question, or an interesting statistic can do the trick.

Step 2 - Identify the problem

Example: *"Mmm, they're good at pooping, but you know who sucks at pooping? You do. That's because when you sit on the porcelain throne, this muscle puts a kink in the hose and stops the Ben and Jerry's from sliding out smoothly. Is that a problem? I don't know, are hemorrhoids a problem? Because sitting at this angle can cause hemorrhoids, bloating, constipation, and a buttload of other crap. Seriously, unicorn hemorrhoids, the glitter gets everywhere. But what happens when you go from a sit to a squat? Violà! This muscle relaxes, and the kink goes away faster then Pegasus laying sweet sorbet dookie. Now your colon's open and ready for battle. That's because our bodies were made to poop in a squat, and now there's a product that lets you squat in your own home."*

Your goal is to make the consumer aware of what the problem is and why it's affecting them. Don't be afraid to "twist the knife" and explain just how badly this problem can affect the consumer. In this ad, they talk about hemorrhoids, bloating, and constipation. This causes the user to self-identify if they've had those issues or if they are things they certainly want to avoid. Users should end this section by being intrigued and interested to learn more about how to solve this problem.

Step 3 - Identify the solution

Example: *"Introducing, the Squatty Potty™. No, Squatty Potty™ is not a joke, and yes, it will give you the best poop of your life, guaranteed. I don't just mean you bloated lords and hemorrhoidal ladies. I mean everyone. Kink, unkink, kink, unkink. It's simple science, really."*

Important point: The solution is meant to solve the problem, not sell your product. The solution must convince the consumer that the problem exists and that the solution is going to solve the problem. This then leads the consumer to convince themselves that your product is the right product to fix the problem.

Step 4 - The guarantee

Example: *"Can't get the last scoop out of the carton? With the Squatty Potty™, you get complete elimination. Spend too much time on the chamber pot? The Squatty Potty™ makes you go twice as fast or your money back. I scream, you scream, and plop plop, baby."*

This is meant to make a promise to the consumer that your product is going to solve their problem.

Step 5 - Results and benefits

Example: *"Maybe you're sore from squeezing out solid globs of rocky road. The Squatty Potty™ gives you a smooth stream of fro-yo that glides like a virgin swan. Plus, when you're done, it tucks neatly out of sight, thanks to its innovative patented design. Truly a footstool fit for a constipated king."*

Quite simply, what will it do for your customers, and why is it different or what are any remaining features that make it unique?

Step 6 - Call to action

Example: *"So, if you're a human being who poops from your butt, click here to order your Squatty Potty™ today at SquattyPotty.com."*

At this point, your viewer/reader should be ready to purchase, so help direct them down the path of purchase. Add a link to your site where they can purchase or tell them where to find your product. Take the guesswork out of the process and be direct.

Step 7 - Social proof

Example: *"You'll wish you tried it years ago, and if you don't trust a prince, how about your doctor?* Shark Tank, Huff Post, NPR, Men's Health, *Howard Stern? He poops from his butt. They're all crazy about the Squatty Potty™. Not to mention the 2,000 Amazon users who gave the Squatty Potty™ five stars. Including the author of this moving haiku: 'Oh Squatty Potty™, you fill me with endless joy yet leave me empty.'"*

If everyone else is using it and finding value, then it's safe to say that you will have a similar experience. Don't over complicate it; just tell your story of the benefits that others are having.

Step 8 - Second call to action

Example: *"So, order your Squatty Potty™ today. I'm not saying it will make you poop as soft as cookies and cream, but I'm not saying it won't. Squatty Potty™, the stool for better stools. Pooping will never be the same and neither will ice cream."*

It's smart to end your pitch with another prompt to action to help move your viewer to buy your product. This may feel redundant but it's proven to work. You typically have to ask for the sale six times before your client finally says "yes." Asking twice in your pitch will help move those folks along who are on the fence by the end of your script.

It is smart to remember that using humor is effective but difficult. It's also important to remember that in this commercial, much of the humor comes from the video and images, facial expressions, and gestures being made in conjunction with the words being said. As we know, what you say is a small part of your overall communication, so think about that point if you are writing a script that is meant to be acted/read out or just written in the form of copy. This makes a big difference in how/if you decide to use humor for your script.

There you have it! Eight steps to help you write a script that can help sell your product or service. While the Squatty Potty™ was a smashing success, it wasn't without risk and its style doesn't fit for every product. Some may use humor, some may be more informative, and so on. I recently created an infomercial and a two-minute video that was informative, educational, positive, and upbeat. Those characteristics fit my style of presenting. If I tried to write a script that was exactly like Squatty Potty™, it wouldn't turn out that great. Be true to yourself and do your best.

Skill-building exercise:

1. Write down the first five topics of content that are to be part of your marketing and promotion plan. Think about the big picture and what you are hoping to convey to the target audience. Is it important to educate your audience first? If that's the case, start there and gradually introduce your product as a solution that the consumer will consider. Start by educating them on the condition, disease, situation, etc. and why this problem exists, as well as how devastating it can be. Review the different problem scenarios, and consider what value can be added with your product/solution.

    If the plan is to create content that sells your product, then you should consider a video that explains the product and how to effectively use it to solve the "problem." That may require one informational video about the simple ways to get started using your product. Start with something that can be used in conjunction with online ads, that is short (less than fifteen to thirty seconds), and that is good to use with Facebook and Instagram.

    Take time to think about the strategy and the next steps to create content that you are comfortable with, and even plan out what topics you want to cover.

Certainly, one of the pieces of content needs to be your sales script. This may be difficult if you don't feel comfortable selling, but at the end of the day, if you don't tell people that it's out there and that they need it, you will never sell anything.

This plan may look like:

1. What is the problem?

2. What is my solution?

3. Who is the target market?

4. What is the key message?

5. Blog or video plan:

    a. scripts

    b. video/photo shoot schedule

    c. blog posting, frequency, timeline, self-posted or posting service, etc.

2. Think about how to sell the product and what the sales video or content will look like and then write copy. Use the sales script example in the previous case study, and put pen to paper. Start writing and just let the ideas flow. Like any great copy, it will not be perfect on the first draft and will continue to be modified and improved over time.

The most important first step is to write down your plans and get started. Once started, you will go back through your plan from time to time and find ways to improve what you're selling and better methods to engage your audience. Start with the expectation that the first version of your plan is a rough draft and doesn't need to be perfect. This may feel unnatural if it's your first attempt to write a marketing plan/sales pitch/script, but it will feel rewarding when you get through the first step, which is the rough draft. Ask for copious amounts of feedback from your spouse, friend, and coworkers. After you develop your marketing plan, you are ready to move on to selling your innovation/invention. Good luck!

References

Blog.wishpond.com. (2019). Tom Fishburne quote. Accessed on March 30, 2019. Accessed at https://blog.wishpond.com/post/70494294231/50-inspirational-marketing-quotes-2013.

Nash, R. & Jang, J. (2015). *Preparing Students for Life Beyond College: A Meaning-Centered Vision for Holistic Teaching and Learning*. Routledge Publisher. New York, NY.

Ferriss, T. (2016). *Tools of Titans: The Tactics, Routines, and Habits of Billionaires, Icons, and World-Class Performers*. Houghton Mifflin Harcourt Publishing. UK.

8 Engaging Nurses in Innovation

By Dr. Bonnie Clipper

Objectives

By the end of this chapter, the reader will be able to:

*   Explain why engaging nurses in innovation is important.

*   Provide examples of activities that can be utilized to engage nurses on the innovation journey.

*   Describe innovation events that will best help advance creative ideas or build a culture of innovation within your organization.

    "Where the needs of the world and your talents cross, there lies your vocation."

    — Aristotle (Nursebuff.com, 2019)

Why engage nurses?

There are currently four million registered nurses (American Nurses Association, 2018), compared to approximately one million physicians, just over 309,000 pharmacists, and nearly 240,000 physical therapists. As the data indicate, nurses represent the largest group of health care workers/clinicians. However, it is not just the sheer number of nurses compared to other health professionals that makes engaging nurses in innovation so important. Nurses are also the profession that spends more time with patients and their families than any other health care discipline. It is both the number of nurses and their consistent interaction with patients that makes nurses the most natural group to participate in innovation as a means to improving the health of our country. Being consistently the "closest" to patients allows nurses to function not only as a strong barometer of the transformation and improvement that needs to occur but also as a gauge to determine the impact and efficacy of innovations.

Even though there are four times as many nurses as the next largest health care professionals (physicians), there is a tendency for nurses to be underrepresented in the innovation space, specifically in the influence, design/development, and testing phases. Being underrepresented is not surprising, considering that nursing remains a female-dominated profession. In fact, 2017 data indicate that nursing remains a profession consisting of 89 percent females, compared to 11 percent males (Auerbach, D., Buerhaus, P., Skinner, L., & Staiger, D., 2017), a statistic indicating only slight growth historical trends. While this is not a complete "apples to apples" comparison, data also demonstrate that governance boards related to STEM (science, technology, engineering, and math) have a disproportionate board composition based on gender, which is demonstrated even when taking the global view. In a 2015 study by Credit Suisse Research Institute (2016), it was identified that on an international level, women on STEM boards comprise 12.2 percent, compared to men representing 87.8 percent of STEM-related company board seats.

While it is an extrapolation, based on this type of data, it is not difficult to see the pattern emerge that nurses are underrepresented in innovation because involvement and equality in engagement starts with the composition and representation of leadership. Nurses also tend to be underrepresented in the development of actual innovations and emerging technologies often due to the resources and investment needed on the front end to develop, prototype, produce, market, and sell new products. Many nurses simply don't have the hefty disposable incomes that their physician counterparts do to advance their work. Additionally, nurses have traditionally not been coached to "lean in" to innovation related conversations and take the lead. This is the perfect time for that to change.

Influencing the development of emerging innovations

Participating on an advisory board or a corporate board is a great way to share nursing expertise, knowledge of patient and family dynamics, and your knowledge of health care workflows. This is often the point where influence can be exerted, as new products and strategic plans are discussed. The opportunity for more nurses to join technology-related corporate or advisory boards can only be viewed as a positive, as nurses are strong advocates for patients and are able to provide valuable insight into the care environment, which can mean technology companies are spending their resources on solving the right problems. To find a corporate or advisory board position, there are two ways to get a jump start: 1) using "six degrees of separation," ask colleagues if they know of an entrepreneur with a start-up company or talk to medical device/technology sales representatives to see if they are aware of any opportunities for you to volunteer, or 2) check out the Nurses on Boards Coalition at NursesOnBoardsCoalition.org. This is a great, non-profit organization dedicated to seeing 10,000 nurses on boards by 2020.

Another way for nurses to influence in the innovation space is during the design and development stages of new devices and technologies. When innovations emerge as a result of product development, it is important that they solve the "right" problem. Often in health care, it seems that solutions/products are being developed for problems that may not really be as big of an issue as they appear to patients or caregivers. While it may be cynical, it can be considered that since there is so much money to be made on health care-related "solutions," there will be a market for every solution, no matter how large or small. As natural problem solvers and pros at understanding health care workflows, nurses should be included to provide input into product design and development to ensure that the "solution" does, in fact, solve the right problem.

Nurses as a profession have an advantage in that they can provide unique insight into not only the problems but also the potential solutions. When thinking about innovation, it is not uncommon for industry representatives (i.e., sales reps) to approach nurse leaders and nurses after the product has been purchased by the organization just to ask them to be a "super-user" or to help roll out the product as part of the implementation team. It is typical for most nurses to have their first touch-point or demo of a product at this time. However, the opportunity to influence product or technology design and development has already passed. Instead, nurses need to push for this process to become inverted and allow nurses the opportunity for input up front, during the design and development phase.

It is pretty common for an organization to purchase new equipment or supplies, and after using them for a short time, the nurses come up with a better, faster, or cheaper way to use the device. By incorporating nursing input through the human-centered design process from the start, this will not only provide a more "nurse-friendly" product but will also allow for a more successful product due to the nurses' familiarity with the patient population and patient care processes. This is yet another reason to participate on an advisory board.

Innovation cannot occur in a vacuum and should be diverse in thought and input. Just as the Five Rights of Medication Administration (right medication, right patient, right dose, right route, and right time) ensure safety (ISMP, 2007), there should also be five rights to innovation in healthcare. These should include: identifying the right problem, settling on the right solution, implementing at the right time, ensuring that the right price allows for scale and sustainability, and ensuring that the right education is rolled out in order to ensure safe and effective rollout.

Five "Rights" of Healthcare Innovation
right problem
right solution
right time
right price
right education

Nurses *are* innovators!

As stated earlier, nursing is the largest group of clinicians compared to their colleagues. Yet it is interesting that nurses do not see themselves as innovators. When I ask a large group of nurses directly if they are innovators, typically only 10-20 percent raise their hands. When the question is changed to ask if any nurses within this group have used "work-arounds" to provide the necessary care to their patients, many hands go up.Finally, when I ask if they have ever had to go so far as to "MacGyver" something to provide care to a patient, most hands in the room are raised. This is innovation! Nurses are natural innovators.

Equally as interesting as the fact that nurses do not see themselves as innovators is the frequency they routinely innovate. In a 2009 study, it was discovered that during an average shift while caring for a patient in a hospital setting, nurses have an average of one "operational failure" per hour, resulting in eight to twelve per shift, depending on shift length (Tucker, 2009). Operational failures are defined as system- or process-related problems that break down and impede the safe or timely provision of care. The concern is, of course, patient safety. However, there are also the issues of cost, timing, effectiveness, and experience that factor into this problem. While the mere fact that "operational failures" exist is concerning, the key takeaway here is that each of these episodes of "operational failure" require a course correction or innovation to occur in order to avoid the untoward event. Even knowing that nurses do this an average once per hour, when asked, nurses do not see themselves as innovators. This must be changed. We need nurses to see themselves as the innovators, inventors, and problem solvers that they are. Each and every nurse has the permission to call themselves an innovator!

> *"Nurses often are natural problem solvers . . . they have been trained to suppress their divergent thinking tendencies."*
>
> — The Innovation Roadmap: A Guide for Nurse Leaders (Cianelli et al. 2016)

How to engage nurses

One way to engage nurses is to educate the entire health care team on what innovation is and how it can be used to solve both internal and external challenges. According to *The Innovation Roadmap: A Guide for Nurse Leaders*, there are many ways to build an engaged team to tackle problems through the use of innovation (Cianelli et al. 2016). This approach helps ensure that as roles and vacancies are filled within the department (or organization), it is done in a way that will help build an engaged and innovative team. Engaging a group of nurses in innovation has strong potential to improve retention, job satisfaction, and a sense of accountability by building a culture of innovation and an ecosystem that supports it. Working to build a culture of innovation includes the following:

- Develop an organizational culture that rewards organizational agility (being nimble).

- Hire employees who are able/willing to quickly adapt to change.

- Develop employee rules and procedures that support agility, change, and flexibility (this can be done through Shared Governance or committee structures).

- Create employee cross-functional/interdisciplinary teams that are readily available to provide input for urgent organizational changes, sort of like a "Change/Innovation" SWAT team.

- Encourage sharing of experiences and storytelling when tackling innovative problem solving. The stories really get to the *empathy* portion of the problem, which is the "true heart" of the issue (Cianelli et al. 2016, 10).

"Innovation is the act that endows resources with a new capacity to create wealth."

— Peter Drucker (Brainyquote, 2018)

Using this approach to develop a strategy to engage nurses in innovation will begin to build a culture where innovation is expected and rewarded. The key to engaging nurses is to provide time for innovative thinking to flourish and to develop a menu of events that will be seen as fun, not as "work." A few innovation-based events, such as an innovation catalyst competition (pitch event), hackathon, or innovation lab-type event, will be described as a place to start.

What is an innovation catalyst competition?

An innovation catalyst competition is a great way to jumpstart ideas through high-energy events. These are also known as a "pitch competitions." The best known and most successful example of this is *Shark Tank*. *Shark Tank* is a very popular, Emmy award-winning television reality show on ABC . This show has been credited with bringing energy to the world of small company entrepreneurship and, due to its success from both a viewership perspective, as well as for entrepreneurs obtaining funding, it is in its tenth season (*Shark Tank*, 2018). *Shark Tank* portrays contestants (entrepreneurs) "pitching" their products to a panel of five judges. The judges are charismatic, successful business people who have made millions or even billions of dollars through their own ideas, start-up businesses, acquisitions, or investments (*Shark Tank*, 2018).

The judges carefully listen to the pitches to determine if they consider the ideas to be solid enough from a business case perspective to warrant their personal investment in the product or concept in order to grow the market share or to further develop the contestant's product or concept with a goal of turning a profit. The judges dialogue with the contestant about the product and ask several questions, including how products are made, what the margins are, how much debt the company has, the plan to increase market share, what specific deal or investment the contestants are looking for, and finally, the percent of equity the business is willing to give up for the investment in their company. Some entrepreneurs are successful in their "ask" from the "Sharks," and some are not. The show provides contestants access to investment capital in ways that they may not otherwise have had (*Shark Tank*, 2018).

Shark Tank is essentially a "pitch" competition, an event that provides opportunities for individual entrepreneurs to develop and present their version of an elevator pitch (hence the term) to inform potential investors or buyers of the product in a short concise pitch. This type of event generates "buzz" and excitement around a challenge, product, or service and helps it become "visible" in the marketplace. Whether the goal is to identify investors or sell products, the excitement is typically a catalyst for the innovator/owner to progress to whatever is the next step of the business. Just like in the television version of *Shark Tank*, there is typically a panel of judges who represent a variety of skills and backgrounds that make the final determinations of the "winners" of the competition. In the nursing community, look for NursePitch™, a pitch event started by the American Nurses Association (American Nurses Association NursePitch, 2019).

Why is this called a pitch challenge? It refers to an event that may or may not have a theme, although it's typically not a deeply specific problem. The goal of innovation catalyst competitions is for nurses or nurse-led teams to advance their ideas and potentially win prize money that can be used to further develop or market their product or concept, or better yet, secure valuable coaching time through an incubator or accelerator. The ability to gain expertise from designers, engineers, and business leaders is invaluable in the early stages of product development and start-up company lifecycles. Why are these events so fun? Not only are they fast-paced and exciting, they are great practice for aspiring entrepreneurs to become proficient at their sixty-second or two-minute pitch delivery to the panel of judges and crowd. Depending on the format, it is fun for the audience too, as there is often input from them to determine the "winners" or a "people's choice" type of award.

Resources for your pitch:

- "The Art of the Pitch" (Kawasaki 2015)

- "How to Write a Business Pitch" (Scribendi 2018)

- "Nine Things That Take a Pitch from Good to Great" (Cummings, n.d.)

Call to Action

Within the next thirty days, search online through the websites of universities (especially those with engineering or bioengineering departments), professional associations (such as the American Nurses Association (ANA) or Health Information and Management Systems Society, aka HIMSS), tech newsletters, or even large medical device companies to determine if there are any innovation catalyst competitions/pitch events in your region that you can submit your creative idea/concept/prototype to. Or if you are not ready to submit your own idea, find an event to attend to observe and learn from the process.

Watch episodes of *Shark Tank* and search for pitch videos to help you write your own pitch. Don't give up, as this is a very hard process to perfect. Attend the event as either a competitor and journal your experience or as an observer and take notes to help sharpen your plan to submit in the future.

Conducting your own innovation catalyst competition/pitch event:

1. Develop a theme for the event (not a specific problem) rather than something general, such as: digital tools to allow seniors to age in place, wearables that improve independent living for stroke patients, etc. A theme is not required for a pitch event, depending on how adventurous the organization is.

2. Determine the event date and time. Market in advance to generate enough interest and a good supply of high-quality contestants. Twelve to sixteen weeks is generally the right amount of time to communicate the theme and begin to solicit applicants. These events can never be marketed "too much"—more marketing is better than less marketing. Also, consider whether there is a local chapter or organization that may be interested in co-sponsoring the event to help get the word out, as well as to receive some of the visibility.

3. Determine how candidates will submit their innovative ideas for a pre-screening process (this often happens via email). The purpose of pre-screening is to ensure that candidates' ideas are appropriate for the goals and theme of the event. Protections around intellectual property (IP) are extremely important as well. One way to do this is to have the candidates ensure that they are an LLC (limited liability company) or can indicate through documentation or a waiver that they have all the necessary intellectual property protections in place. This is important since the product or service will be pitched and demonstrated in front of a live audience, where it is not feasible that all attendees sign an NDA (non-disclosure agreement). If there are questions, it is always safer to consult a legal expert in advance in this area.

4. It always helps to secure some type of prize money, no matter how small. This can be accomplished through sponsorship or partnership through appropriate industry, college, or vendor relationships. Be mindful of all organizational ethics and compliance requirements, as well as laws that pertain to event sponsorship.

5. Secure adequate space, including seating and display space for the pitch competition so the audience can easily watch, as well as space for the innovation contestants' products or informational posters.

6. Secure AV equipment, such as: screen, projector, and microphones. The crowd will need to see and hear the pitch.

7. Secure a panel of three to five judges. These can be local "celebrities," association presidents, VC's, device or innovation experts, faculty, etc. The goal is to identify credible judges who will not only be selecting the winner but also asking insightful and provocative questions throughout the event. The goal is for the pitch competitors to learn how to improve their pitch and their product.

8. Communicate the results after the event, whether through press releases, social media, websites, or both. The more visibility that winners and contestants receive, the better. Live streaming is always an exciting way to conduct these events.

9. Consider a registration process for attendees so there is a head count and knowledge of who is in the audience. It is important to know if there are potential funders who may want to connect with participants. This will also help determine the level of interest for future events.

"Innovation is taking two things that already exist and putting them together in a new way."

— Tom Freston (Brainyquote, 2018)

What is a hackathon/code-a-thon?

Hackathons and code-a-thons are similar events. They utilize a problem or challenge as the theme of the event and ask attendees to come up with solutions for the specific challenge or problem in a fixed amount of time. Hackathons/code-a-thons are known as a reverse pitch event because there is a specific problem that the group is working to solve. For example, a "code-a-thon to use big data to improve health disparities" is intentionally bringing together a group to collaborate with the goal of solving or making a sizeable dent toward resolving the detailed problem.

These events can be small and contained within a department or company, or they can be large and include attendees from a regional, national, or international reach. Some hackathons/code-a-thons can include hundreds or even thousands of attendees and be held in large conference centers for breakout-type topics over one, two, or three days. There are large Hackathon/code-a-thon events that extend over several days that actually provide access to sleep rooms in hour-long increments in order to allow attendees access to rest while they continue to literally work through the night (or nights) to actively resolve a problem or challenge. This approach is not ideal because in order to be at your best, sleep, food, and a hot shower are important.

Hackathons/code-a-thons are intended for high-energy, rigorous, active problem-solving and dialogue; access to your laptop is essential, as it is not uncommon for teams to be divided up around particular aspects of a problem or solution and for each individual on the team to have a unique skill or role in the solution process. While the terms "hackathon" and "code-a-thon" are often used synonymously, the difference is that a hackathon is often more generic and may include actual computers and tech talent "hacking" information, while a code-a-thon is typically reserved for computer, big data, and informatics solutions. Both are rewarding to be a part of.

While these types of events generate a buzz and have produced good solutions, it is important to keep up the momentum after the event. Remember that the goal of hackathons/code-a-thons is to solve a problem, even if it is in the smallest, most incremental way. Disruptive innovation is not impossible, although not likely in this format. Having said that, it is important to work each solution through the proper pilots and filters to be sure that the solutions really do what they are expected to and have the desired impact. As lessons are learned from the pilot projects, iterations or "tweaks" may be necessary to refine the solutions to the point that they are consistently successful. One of the most important features of hackathons/code-a-thons is to broadly communicate and widely disseminate, to all participants, the outcomes of the hackathons/code-a-thons and any solutions that were part of the outcome, along with the results of any pilot projects.

This is a great chance for associations, professional organizations, nursing schools and other nursing-related groups to make an impact. The more the results of hackathons/code-a-thons can be shared and disseminated, the better it is for their success and visibility. Participants are more willing to participate when there is a goal and shared outcome of these kinds of events. However, one caveat is to be careful of any intellectual property, as this should always be protected prior to sharing any solutions, especially if it can be monetized. If the intellectual property is a result of a large group effort, it is possible that it can still be protected and shared in an open source manner. It is suggested that legal experts in the area of intellectual property be consulted prior to sharing any IP that can be monetized.

Examples: There have been hackathons/code-a-thons around a multitude of topics. In the past year, the most common topic in healthcare seems to be opioid addiction issues. The result of a few of these activities is that they are disseminated through a variety or professional associations.

Conducting your own hackathon/code-a-thon event:

1. Develop a specific challenge for the event, such as: positively impacting the opioid crisis through data, using big data to reduce health disparities, incorporating wearables into the daily life of diabetics, etc.

2. Secure adequate space, including seating and tables, for teams to spread out comfortably.

3. Determine the event date and time. Market in advance to generate enough interest and a good supply of participants. Ten to twelve weeks is generally a good amount of time to communicate the theme and begin to solicit applicants. More time to plan is nearly always better. These can never be marketed "too much"—more marketing is better than less marketing. Also, consider whether there is a local chapter or organization that may be interested in co-sponsoring the event to help get the word out, as well as to receive some of the visibility.

4. Identify mentors for the event, a handful at the minimum who have had previous experience or subject matter expertise to circulate among the teams to offer help and keep things moving at all times. The worst thing in a hackathon or code-a-thon is a lull that kills the creativity and changes the energy to draining instead of upbeat and creative.

5. Consider sponsorship if the event is to involve food or if there is a cost to the space and equipment. Be mindful of all organizational ethics and compliance requirements, as well as laws that pertain to sponsorship. Consult legal counsel to be safe.

6. Consider how to register participants. Several free online solutions are available for this, or it could be through good, old-fashioned email.

7. Secure AV equipment, if needed, such as: screen, projector, and microphones.

8. Communicate the results after the event, whether through press releases, social media, websites, or both. The more visibility that the hackathon and the outcome receives, the better.

Resources for hackathons:

"Ten Tips to Win Your Next Hackathon" (Marie 2017)
"Hackathon Guide" (Tauberer, n.d.)

Call to Action

Within the next sixty days, secure permission to begin conversations on how your organization can use innovation-related events to advance the goals of the organization. Whether through a shared governance committee, employee engagement committee or organizational council, begin to have conversations that might inspire collaborative problem solving. Discuss which type of innovation event (innovation catalyst/pitch competition or hackathon/code-a-thon) is best for your organization, and develop a plan to advance this idea to your organization's decision makers, with a target of actually organizing and implementing one event within the next year.

A high-level leader can help champion this work and move it along within the organization. Cross-functional, interdisciplinary teams are the best approach to soliciting problem solving from everyone, as it will require everyone to help address the goals of the entire organization.

"O! for a muse of fire, that would ascend the brightest heaven of invention."

— William Shakespeare (brainyquote, 2018)

What is an innovation lab?

Typically, an innovation lab is the space where nurses, nurse-led teams, and all disciplines can ideate, create, sketch, or prototype their big ideas and concepts. Depending on the degree of sophistication or even staffing of the innovation lab, there might even be designers or engineers available to assist with the development of concepts into prototypes. In recent years, more professional associations are offering innovation labs as part of their conference experience.

Case study of an organizational exemplar

- Maker Nurse™/Maker Health™, to see how they have handled their Maker Spaces™ (MakerNurse.com)
- The Ohio State University, School of Nursing's Innovation Studio (nursing.osu.edu/sections/office-of-innovation-and-strategic-partnerships/innovation-studio)
- The American Nurses Association Innovation Labs (at their conferences)

  1. Review these websites.
  2. Look at how these innovation labs are using their resources and what is being created in the space.
  3. What are the pros and cons of such a space?
  4. How could this concept work in your organization?

Typically, these types of spaces are called labs or "maker spaces" because of the creative, hands-on work that occurs in them. These spaces are equipped with design and prototyping kinds of equipment, such as laser printers, 3D printers, lathes, whiteboards, power tools, and materials such as PVC pipes, clay, foam blocks, glues, cardboard, pipe cleaners, adhesives, "pleather," velcro, hinges, articulating joints, pulleys, rope, etc. These endeavors can be costly, so check to see if your organization has any funding through a grant or foundation to offset the necessary expenses.

How to create an innovation lab or maker type space:

1. Determine location. Space is often the biggest obstacle to overcome when planning for an inno-vation lab or maker-type space, even if it is temporary. Ensure that the size is adequate enough for people, staff, and equipment to safely operate. It is also important to have adequate ventila-tion if adhesives are to be used and to accommodate for noise issues from power tools. Safety is paramount to the development and use of this type of space. Be sure that it is accessible and easy to get to, with good foot traffic not too far away.

2. Consult designers and/or engineers to determine the best type of equipment for the innovation space. Depending on the goals, it may contain 3D printers, software for blueprints or potentially, materials such as PVC piping, glue, hinges, velcro, tubes, dowels, etc. Innovation labs are all different and depending on the funding, will have access to different equipment and materi-als. If there is access to engineering or biomedical engineer schools/departments, this can be a valuable collaboration to advance the work of this space, as well as to provide expertise and potentially, staffing or support.

3. Determine date(s) and time(s). Innovation labs/spaces require ongoing communication, as the goal is to have people use this space and develop their ideas on a regular basis. More marketing is better than less marketing. Again, consider whether there are other schools, departments, or local chapters/organizations that may be interested in collaborating to help get the word out, support the space, and benefit from some of the visibility.

4. Consider a registration process for attendees, so there is a headcount to allow for staffing of the innovation lab space. This is not necessary, although nice to have in advance. Many organizations affiliated with schools, colleges, or universities may be interested in having students visit the lab.

5. Determine how this will be staffed and who will pay for it. The space should not be open access without someone in attendance who knows how to use the equipment and/or machinery due to the safety implications. Is there access to a university/college, school, or other departments that have design or engineering expertise? There are innovation labs that are able to staff through volunteer engineer or design students; this may be an option to explore if funding is an issue. It is not uncommon to identify a retired engineer or designer looking to volunteer nominal time each week.

6. Determine who will own the intellectual property developed or prototyped in the innovation lab. This is an extremely important point to hammer out in advance of opening. All organizations are different; some indicate that *all* IP is owned by the organization if developed by an employee at

any time. Other organizations may share the ownership of the IP if developed by an employee or employees. Academic institutions tend to have a different take on this. If there are questions, it is always safer to consult a legal expert in this area prior to the set up and operation of an innovation lab type space. Seek legal counsel on this before anything is created in the lab. Make this information clear to all who attend the lab space, in order to avoid conflict later.

Resources for Innovation Labs

"Starting an Innovation Lab? Avoid These Pitfalls" (Tucker 2017).
InnovatorsCompass.org (Ben-Ur, 2019) is a great resource for all things innovation related.

Engaging nurses in innovation is about more than just fun and exhilarating events to stimulate their creative minds. It is about bringing nurses into this space to help them learn and feel comfortable. This is the space where nurses help to prop up other nurses. Failing is part of the fun of the innovation world, is encouraged, and should be celebrated in fun ways. Being willing to develop your idea into a concept and eventually a prototype is a powerful feeling for nurses who are so often left on the sidelines of such conversations. The world is no longer left to the largest corporations to be the only ones who innovate and make money developing and selling products. Helping nurses learn how to advance their work and speak the language of innovation is a way to help them become successful entrepreneurs and small business owners, as well as a key way to transform health and patient outcomes.

Look for ways to get yourself involved and to move your unit, department, or organization in the direction of innovation. It is good to want to ensure health and wellness for a population of people, to improve the way that care is delivered, to improve how patients experience their care, and how our nursing practice occurs, as well as to make money doing so. It is not a mutually exclusive equation. Branch out, put your ideas on paper, and take a risk in developing them—become an entreprenurse! The world needs to hear what nurses have to say and see what nurses have to offer.

References

American Nurses Association. Accessed on September 8, 2018. Accessed at https://www.nursingworld.org/.
American Nurses Association Nurse Pitch. (2019). Accessed on February 23, 2019. Accessed at http://pteqicon.org/2019-program/nurse-pitch/.
Ben-Ur, E. (2019). Innovators Compass Tools. Accessed on March 19, 2019. Accessed at http://InnovatorsCompass.org.
Bplans. (2018). Nine Things That Take a Pitch From Good to Great. Accessed on September 20, 2018. Accessed at https://articles.bplans.com/9-things-that-take-a-pitch-from-good-to-great.

Brainyquote. (2018). Accessed on July 15, 2018. Accessed at https://www.brainyquote.com/topics/innovation.

Brainyquote. (2018). Accessed on July 15, 2018. Accessed at https://www.brainyquote.com/topics/innovation.

Brainyquote. (2018). Accessed on July 15, 2018. Accessed at https://www.brainyquote.com/topics/invention.

Cianelli, R., Clipper, B., Freeman, R., Goldstein, J. & Wyatt, T. (2016). *The Innovation Road Map: A Guide for Nurse Leaders*. Greensboro, NC. Published by Innovation Works.

Clipper, B. & Dawson, J. (February, 2018), *Innovation Series: Key Competencies for Nursing*. American Nurse Today. 13(2), pp. 24.

Credit Suisse Research Institute. (2016). The CS Gender 3000: The Reward for Change. p. 9. Accessed on September 9, 2018. Accessed at http://publications.credit-suisse.com/?referralUrl=http%3A%2F%2Fpublications%2Ecredit-suisse%2Ecom%2Findex%2Ecfm%2Fpublikationen-shop%2Fresearch-institute%2Fcs-gender-3000%2F.

Debono, D., Greenfield, D., Travaglia, J., Long, J., Black, D., Johnson, J. & Braithwaite, J. (2013). Nurses' workarounds in acute healthcare settings: a scoping review. BMC Health Services Research. (13) 175, pp. 1-16.

Forbes. (2017). Starting an Innovation Lab. Accessed on September 20, 2018. Accessed at https://www.forbes.com/sites/robertbtucker/2017/11/20/starting-an-innovation-lab-avoid-these-pitfalls/#68262be87a2b.

Girls Know Tech (2017). Accessed on September 20, 2018. Accessed at https://girlknowstech.com/10-tips-win-hackathon.

ISMP. (January 25, 2007) The five rights: A destination without a map. ISMP Medication Safety Alert. 12(2). Accessed on August 28, 2018. Accessed at http://www.ihi.org/resources/Pages/ImprovementStories/FiveRightsofMedicationAdministration.aspx.

Kawasaki, G. (2015). The Art of the Pitch. Accessed on September 20, 2018. Accessed at https://guykawasaki.com/the-art-of-the-pitch.

Moore, E. (August, 2018). Innovation Needs Nurses. American Nurse Today. 13(8), p. 35.

Nursebuff.com. (2019). Aristotle quote. Accessed on March 30, 2019. Accessed at https://www.nursebuff.com/nursing-quotes-2/.

Nurses on Boards Coalition (2018). Accessed on January 18, 2019. Accessed at https://www.nursesonboardscoalition.org/.

Nursingworld.org. (2019). NursePitch™. Accessed on February 23, 2019. Accessed at http://pteqicon.org/2019-program/nurse-pitch.

Shark Tank. (2018). Accessed on August 11. Accessed at https://abc.go.com/shows/shark-tank.

Tauberer, J. (2018). Hackathon Guide. Accessed on September 20, 2018. Accessed at https://hackathon.guide.

Young, A., Chaudhry, H. J., Pei, X., Arnhart, K., Dugan, M. & Snyder, G. B. (2016). A Census of Actively Licensed Physicians in the United States. Journal of Medical Regulation, 103(2), pp. 7-21.

9   Conclusion

By Dr. Bonnie Clipper

Without trust, the most essential element of innovation—conflict— becomes impossible.

— Patrick Lencioni. (Brainyquote 2018)

It cannot be overstated the role that nurses play and will continue to play in transforming the health and wellbeing of our country, and even of the world. As the caregivers closest to patients and their families, nurses are often the most familiar with workflows, systems issues, and challenges that get in the way of providing the best care, education, and prevention strategies possible.

By tapping into the expertise and knowledge of nurses and their natural skill set of innovation, we will trailblaze a path forward, where nurses lead the transformation of not only care but also health. The innovations and creative thinking of nurses will produce not only new devices and technologies but also unique new models of care that can be adapted or iterated as necessary for a variety of health care organizations and communities, not to mention customized options for each patient.

By coming together to write this book, we had a set of goals that we wanted to positively impact and which are important to our team. These include increasing the number of nurses:

- serving on advisory boards for innovative companies,

- providing input into the design and development of new products and models of care,

- writing business plans through Lean Canvas and starting companies,

- inventing and commercializing new gizmos, gadgets, and devices, as well as approaches to reducing disparities and health inequities,

- developing an innovator's mindset and becoming entreprenurses,

- securing funding for products that will generate revenue,

- blowing away competitors through amazing marketing, and

- using innovation and design thinking as creative and collaborative problem-solving tools.

Using the tools and strategies described in this book will allow aspiring nurse innovators and even nurse leaders to boldly advance their ideas, build prototypes or models, or even develop business plans that could lead to securing funding for the next million-dollar idea. This is exciting stuff, and if you are like each of us, it will keep you up at night—in a good way.

Nurses are the greatest of all innovators, yet don't see themselves as such because they do what they need to in order to provide the very best care for their patients. After all, isn't this why we went to school to become a nurse? Whether it is a workaround or a MacGyver moment, nurses as innovators have much to offer, not only in terms of real solutions but also in terms of innovations that can be commercialized and monetized.

There is no shame in generating money doing what you are most passionate about, and many nurses have done it successfully. Why not make money doing what you love? Maybe it is a side hustle, or perhaps it will become your full-time job. It is hard work and never stops, but it isn't exhausting because you will love it. Learning the lessons of this book and putting them into practice will help nurses advance their ideas in a way that not only will solve the challenges that we encounter on a regular basis but will also help bring recognition for the amazingly innovative work that nurses do.

The ability to be inventors, creators, and problem solvers, along with the fact that we remain the most trusted professionals for seventeen years now (Gallup.com, 2018) is a powerful combination that cannot be matched or rivaled by any other profession. We need the collective support of four million registered nurses to work together, advocate, and champion the transformation of health through nurse-led innovation.

We got together to write this book because none of us had this resource when we started our own journey. We had to figure out every step the hard way, calling friends, looking online, sounding unconfident and insecure in our pitches, and asking for funding. Our objective was to produce a toolkit, or how-to guide, that will assist *you* in advancing *your* ideas and helping *your* organization build successful cultures of innovation. This book has been our way to share with you the awesome feeling of creating something that you are passionate about, starting a business, and selling something that you "invented" and marketed to an audience. We want you to carry this book with you at all times, dog-ear it, write in it, circle things, cross out the parts you don't like, highlight the stuff you do like and stuff into your bag on a daily basis. Use this book to write down your ideas, sketch out your business plan, and jot down the names and number of new contacts who can help you advance and monetize your idea. Everyone on our team still carries a notebook or journal to serve this purpose.

This book has been a labor of love and is the first of its kind, a book on innovation written for nurses, by nurses. We were purposeful about this work and even challenged ourselves to continue to innovate while writing it. The story of our team is that each member is a unique nurse innovator in their own right and has their "bruises" and stories to prove it. We call them our "war" stories, and they are best told over an adult beverage. Our amazing team has a total of 108 years in nursing, forty-nine years as innovators/entrepreneurs, a total of fourteen patents or pending patents, and eighteen trademarks or pending trademarks.

We came together around this topic and felt like a team from the very first conversation at a trade show, through our text introductions and regular phone calls. Our journey is the same as the lessons we share with you, although yours should hopefully be smoother. We have not executed every step perfectly, and we want to help you avoid the same mistakes by sharing "how to do" things. By writing this book, we believe that we are shortening your "launch to success" trajectory and saving you a few hassles and headaches. Our team consists of nurse practitioners, nurse executives, and direct care nurses. We are all sought out as thought leaders in the innovation space and proud to share our experiences and expertise to help other nurses as we "pass the torch" (a nod to Florence there) and advance nurse-led innovation.

We suggest that you learn all that you can and read often about other innovators, both inside and outside of healthcare. Attend as many Hackathons, NursePitch™ events, conferences, and Innovation Catalyst Competitions that you can. Watch *Shark Tank,* and learn how to deliver your pitch in five minutes and then within one minute. Perfect your elevator pitch. Who knows when the next person you deliver it to will be a potential funder or partner. Learn, learn, learn. Find a mentor or several mentors, and capture their thoughts to help you stay on track. Share your successes with us. We are all active on social media and would love to hear your stories.

Our team of nurse innovators are not the only nurse innovators around and are certainly not legal experts, so we always suggest that you develop a relationship with an attorney with expertise in intellectual property, one whom you can talk to regularly as needed. This book is NOT a substitute for legal advice. Really. Read your employee handbook, and read what you sign—don't give your work away unknowingly. While we aren't legal experts, we have developed several successful products, built and sold successful businesses, advanced cutting-edge work in nursing innovation, and have continued on the exciting journey to improve care across our country. And while aspirational, we all want to transform health along the way.

Thank you and happy innovating!

"It always seems impossible, until it is done."

— Nelson Mandela (Brainy Quote, 2018)

References

Brainy Quote. (2018). Nelson mandela. Accessed on February 23, 2019. Accessed at https://www.brainyquote.com/quotes/nelson_mandela_378967.

Brainy Quote. (2018). Peter lencioni. Accessed on February 23, 2019. Accessed at https://www.brainyquote.com/quotes/patrick_lencioni_834091.

Gallup.com. (2018). Nurses Again Outpace Other Professions for Honesty, Ethics. Accessed on March 18, 2019. Accessed at https://news.gallup.com/poll/245597/nurses-again-outpace-professions-honesty-ethics.aspx.

Dr. Bonnie Clipper, DNP, RN, MA, MBA, CENP, FACHE, is the chief clinical officer at Wambi, an employee engagement and patient empowerment platform. She was previously the vice president of innovation at the American Nurses Association. She has spent more than twenty years in executive nursing roles and transitioning over the past four years to focus on innovation. She speaks internationally on topics of innovation and emerging technologies impacting nursing. Dr. Clipper is a Robert Wood Johnson Executive Nurse Fellow alumna and an ASU/AONE Executive Fellow in Health Innovation Leadership alumna. Her research interests include building cultures of innovation and importing the voice of the nurse into the design and development of technology. She has published on the impact of robots on nursing practice, authoring the book, *The Nurse Manager's Guide to an Intergenerational Workforce*, and co-authoring, *The Innovation Roadmap: A Guide for Nurse Leaders*. Bonnie can be followed @ThoughtleaderRN.

Michael Wang, MSN, RN, APRN, is the CEO and founder of Inspiren, an award-winning healthcare technology company. After serving honorably in the United States Army, he returned to school to become a nurse and ultimately, a nurse practitioner. Wang held numerous roles at New York-Presbyterian Hospital and has vast clinical experience in cardiothoracic surgery and direct patient care. In addition, he holds numerous patents on innovative technologies in both the healthcare and hospitality industry and has founded two successful companies prior to Inspiren. Wang received a bachelor's degree from Emory University, majoring in biology and sociology. He attended graduate school at Columbia University, studying both business and nursing. In 2018, Wang was awarded Fast Company's Innovation by Design Award for his work in leading the creation of iN, Inspiren's flagship solution.

Dr. Paul Coyne, DNP, RN, MBA, MS, APRN, AGPCNP-BC was forced out on disability from his career at Goldman Sachs after the residual effects of a stroke at the age of twenty-six. He then decided to transition into a career in healthcare. His vast work experience spans from serving as manager of analytics at New York-Presbyterian Hospital to leading Advanced Practice Nursing and Clinical Informatics at the Hospital for Special Surgery. Dr. Paul Coyne is now a board-certified adult-gerontology nurse practitioner and president and co-founder of Inspiren, an award-winning healthcare technology company. His success has been recognized nationally, including him being named to Becker's Rising Stars, Healthcare Leaders Under 40, in 2018. Dr. Coyne holds a doctorate, a master's, and a bachelor's degree in nursing from Columbia University, an MBA in healthcare management, a master's in finance from Northeastern University, and a bachelor of arts degree from Providence College. He lives in New York City with his wife, Danialle. Paul can be followed @PaulECoyne.

Vince Baiera, BSN, started his nursing career at The Cleveland Clinic in the Cardiovascular ICU. He then went on to work at Duke University Hospital in the Cardiothoracic ICU before starting to work as a traveling nurse. After traveling the country working as an ICU nurse, Baiera started teaching at Central Nursing College in both theory and clinical rotations. He then transitioned to the business side of healthcare and now works with Straightaway, a software and e-learning company in Long Term Care. Baiera also started his own product development company called Baiera Wellness Products, where the goal is to find innovative ways to serve the many. After his first product, the step2bed™, became a nationwide hit, Baiera began expanding his product offering to focus on products for seniors to help promote wellness and aging-in-place. Baiera resides in San Diego, California, and is currently working on partnerships for expanding his business internationally. Vince can be followed @Vincebaiera.

Rebecca Love, MSN, RN, FIEL, is a nurse entrepreneur, inventor, and TedX speaker and was the first nurse featured on Ted.com and a part of the inaugural nursing panel at SXSW 2018. Rebecca was the first director of Nurse Innovation & Entrepreneurship in the United States at Northeastern School of Nursing, the founding initiative in the country designed to empower nurses as innovators and entrepreneurs. Love also founded the Nurse Hackathon, a movement that has led to transformational change in the nursing profession. She is an experienced nurse entrepreneur, founding HireNurses.com in 2013, which was acquired in 2018. She currently serves as the managing director of US markets for Ryalto. In early 2019, Love, along with a group of leading nurses in the world, founded SONSIEL, The Society of Nurse Scientists, Innovators, Entrepreneurs & Leaders. She is passionate about empowering nurses and creating communities to help nurses innovate, create, and collaborate to start businesses and inventions to transform healthcare. Love can be found @NurseInnovation.

Dawn Drury Nix, BSN, RN, BA, is a native of Clinton, Louisiana, and a cofounder of RNvention, LLC. She holds two degrees from Louisiana State University: a Bachelor of Liberal Arts in French studies and a Bachelor of Science in nursing. Nix has extensive experience in neonatal and pediatric services, working in specialties including pediatric emergency room, pediatric intensive and cardiac care units, and neonatal intensive care, where she currently practices nursing. She is a member of Sigma Theta Tau International Honor Society of Nursing and The Honor Society of Phi Kappa Phi. A skilled educator, Nix serves as a neonatal intensive care unit preceptor and currently aids the management and educational programming of clinical rotations. With her husband, Wayne, she fulfills a chief operating officer role for RNvention and continues to spearhead marketing awareness and outreach efforts for The MultiNix utility tool.

Wayne Nix, MBA, RN, RRT has a mission to innovate! Working in healthcare for over twenty years, he and his wife, Dawn, formed their company, RNvention, LLC, to promote this passion. Nix possesses several degrees, including a master's in business administration, nursing, respiratory, and cardiopulmonary therapy. He specialized most of his clinical career in neonatal and pediatric intensive care, as well as fulfilling several leadership and administrative roles. He also served in the Army National Guard, to which he attributes learning his discipline, grit, and resilience skills. In 2015, Nix received investment funding and over a span of three years, obtained one utility patent, secured two trademarks, won several pitch events, and is currently working to license his product, The MultiNix Tool, a utility tool for nurses. He has consulted on topics such as innovation, commercialization, manufacturing, pitching, business startup advice, event speaking, and select marketing services. Nix can be followed @RNvention.

Dr. Brian Weirich, DHA, RN, MHA, CENP, is a chief nursing officer for Indiana University Health Arnett Hospital and a startup founder. As an innovator with healthcare roles at five nationally ranked health systems, he has worked with some of the world's leading healthcare experts. Dr. Weirich is passionate about reimagining the current state of healthcare, specifically, uniting technology and clinicians to ensure improved patient safety and outcomes. In 2014, he became active at the state and national level by holding board positions and driving industry changes. He is an author/speaker championing the importance of the millennial "tech" generation. In 2017, Dr. Weirich began exploring artificial intelligence and crowdsourcing, as well as the benefits of the gig economy to solve workforce problems. This passion spawned two startup companies that leverage technology to eliminate medication errors and increase access to care. He is a recipient of the Advancement in Medicine grant from the IU School of Medicine and is a founding member of the Society of Nurse Scientists, Innovators, Entrepreneurs & Leaders. Dr. Weirich can be found @BrianWeirichRN.